BRUISED PASSPORTS

BRUISED PASSPORTS

TRAVELLING *the* WORLD *as*
DIGITAL NOMADS

SAVI AND VID

HarperCollins *Publishers* India

First published in India by HarperCollins *Publishers* 2022
4th Floor, Tower A, Building No. 10, Phase II, DLF Cyber City,
Gurugram, Haryana –122002
www.harpercollins.co.in

2 4 6 8 10 9 7 5 3 1

P-ISBN: 978-93-5489-399-5
E-ISBN: 978-93-5489-406-0

Cover design: Devangana Dash
Cover photographs: Savi Munjal and Vidit Taneja

Typeset in 12/16.5 Adobe Garamond at
Manipal Technologies Limited, Manipal

Printed and bound at
Thomson Press (India) Ltd

HarperCollinsIn

We slide into bed after bed after bed ...

Just yesterday we were on a small island off the east coast of Africa, and today in the European hinterland.

Amsterdam, Addis Ababa, Antigua – they all melt into each other and yet remain distinct.

I turn around and feel his familiar breath, still laced with last night's red, on the nape of my neck. I bury myself deeper into covers.

'How did we get here?' I ask.

How?

CONTENTS

Part 2: Trips to Last a Lifetime

Part 3: Living like Digital Nomads

Part 4: Romantic Trips

PROLOGUE

Starry Skies

It's one of those early mornings that make you think – the kind where your mind just unravels. Here in the Finnish wilderness, the sun is yet to rise, even though it's almost 6 a.m. I look up and see thousands of stars etched on the sky over our heads. Suddenly, I see a glimmer of green and before I know it, it's gone. *Are my eyes playing tricks on me?* I wonder! But there it is again, a faint streak of green in the sky, almost like the trail of a shooting star – there one minute, gone the next.

'Get up, get up, I think I saw the Northern Lights,' I whisper cautiously, as if the magic will disappear if I am too loud. But it seems the skies hadn't heard me. Because the heavens burst into a psychedelic party of greens, purples and pinks just as his eyes turn towards the transparent ceiling.

There is something surreal about witnessing the Northern Lights that cannot be put in words. Powdery green lights dancing over our heads one minute disappear the next. Flashes of purple metamorphose into glowing green arches. They twinkle and disappear, reappear and dance right in front of our eyes. There's nothing we can do, except stare. The vibrancy of the colours makes me think the sky is glowing from within. They're neon-green, lime-green, violet and pink all at once.

A tear rolls down my face … this show is getting crazier by the second. And the immensity of the situation strikes me – two little humans, curled up in ivory sheets staring at the mighty Northern Lights from a transparent glass igloo at the Arctic Circle. I lie in the nook of his arm for hours, skin on skin, enjoying the greatest show known to mankind. Our igloo is the first one in a queue of rotund 'hotel rooms'. This is no regular hotel room – it's a transparent igloo with thermal heating. It boasts of beds that can be converted to reclining cinema-style loungers to facilitate nightly viewing of the mysterious Northern Lights.

Growing up in Delhi, India, in the nineties ensured that this wasn't how either of us had envisioned our futures. The only time I would stare at the sky is when I would be begging the gods for a much-needed bout of rain. Air conditioners were a luxury reserved for the 1 per cent. For us, long sweltering days were usually spent guzzling down icy water or nibbling on cooling rose-flavoured concoctions. The lazy whirring of fans provided a welcome sound track to the humdrum of life – history lessons that needed to be read, mathematical tables that needed to be learnt, the scoldings, and the sweet treats, that would inevitably follow.

As a child, I learnt to cherish that gentle drone of fans. Not because the ceiling fan was a novelty, but because we were only too familiar with power cuts! No ordinary power cuts either – these would span six hours, sometimes eight.

'When the electricity went out in our locality, my dad would treat us to ice lollies followed by bedside stories, just to lull us to sleep in the cloying heat. Or else we wouldn't make it to school on time,' I reminisce, sitting in an igloo surrounded by snow.

'At least you had bedside stories for solace,' Vid murmurs. 'I remember carrying mattresses to our terrace in Delhi as a ten-year-old. We had just one pedestal fan on the terrace, between the four of us, and as the youngest, most pampered member of the family, I always managed to score a spot right next to it. During power cuts, I would get stewed in the heat, but I would gaze at the stars with a stupid grin on my face till I fell asleep, safe in the knowledge that I'd be right next to the fan, when the electricity did make an appearance.'

The Northern Lights are beginning to fade, but our eyes continue to be glazed with wonder. I hear Vid's words. I see droplets of water turn to icicles on the walls of our igloo. But all this talk of starlit skies has transported me to the week we spent exploring the deserts of Jordan.

We keep going deeper and deeper into the sandy expanse till the markers of civilization begin to fade away. All we can feel are warm gusts of wind, pieces of gritty sand against our faces, and the gorgeous deep blue sky as we arrive at a ramshackle camp in the middle of nowhere. Our Bedouin guide insists it is the best place to observe night skies in all of Jordan. I look up and see symmetric sand dunes, stretching around us for miles. We tiptoe inside our tent and see two stiff mattresses laid out next to a hookah and an *ibrik*, a traditional Arabic jug.

As we lay down to stretch our tired limbs, I spy the desert sun through the gaping tent. I don't know if it's the unyielding mattress or the dust storm brewing in the valley, but I find myself questioning our decision to sleep in the wilderness. The skies are changing colour. The setting sun casts a warm glow on the dunes. Perhaps it was the tiredness of the day but I wasn't impressed. I organize my luggage, freshen up for dinner, grab some dates and crawl out of our tent.

And that's when I see it. The night sky littered with millions of stars. I keep staring at the staggeringly beautiful sight, too mesmerized to move.

Hours later, we huddle around a small fire smoking hookahs and singing songs with our host. We exchange notes about our adventures, big and small. He tells us why Bedouins worship the nomadic way of life. And then he recites an ancient proverb his parents passed onto him – *When you sleep in a house, your aims are as high as the ceiling; when you sleep outside, they are as high as the stars.*

I don't know if it's this memory about Jordan's night skies, mixed with nostalgia about the unrelenting Indian summers, anecdotes from our childhood, or snow-covered trees practically glowing under the morning sun, but here in the Finnish wilderness, the air feels heady, the moment infinite. Perhaps it's a concoction of everything.

We clothe ourselves warmly from top to toe in woollens – hats, merino-wool thermals, puffer jackets, heat generating socks and snow boots. It's -30°C outside and we want to take no chances. We creep out guardedly, one step at a time, to drink in the sight of dawn in an Arctic forest, close to the northernmost tip of mainland Europe.

In the distance, we spot a baby reindeer nuzzling its mom. I'm in raptures – playing in the snow, chasing sunbeams and dreaming of mythical woodland creatures – even before we've had a chance to explore. We stare at the beams of sunlight filtering through slanting Arctic trees and entire fields covered with glistening snow. The landscape might be laden with snow but we're melting – we can't quite believe the world is home to places such as this!

We spend our days tobogganing down ice-slides, taking long walks in the snow, feasting on warm lingonberry juice – a local speciality – and pelting each other with snow. Even with the below-freezing-point temperatures, the blanket of pure white snow and endless stunning panoramas ensure we spend minimal time indoors. The landscape is peppered with reindeer farms, picturesque trees, igloos and skiing slopes. During our time there we nuzzle husky dogs and snowmobile across frozen rivers. Every day we cross the Arctic wilderness on a sleigh. Sometimes, even when it isn't snowing, a gentle breeze sprinkles a generous helping of snowflakes off the trees onto our faces – a blessing from the heavens above?

We traipse to neighbouring reindeer farms, seduced by the thought of lingering conversations with Sami tribesmen, indigenous people living at the very northern tip of Europe. As we help them herd reindeer, we learn more about their routine. Each day deepens our understanding of the organic matrix of life in this corner of the world. Population is scarce and the nearest neighbour is often five kilometres away. Perhaps that's why nature, human beings and animals coexist in a way we've rarely seen before. Sami herders have long, loving conversations with their reindeer. They worship their food. They sing to the sky and treat it with the reverence it deserves. Sami folklore seamlessly connects the ground and sky because it maintains that the Northern Lights were created from water ejected by the whales. Elsewhere in the region, Norse mythology insists that twinkling stars and the Northern Lights are reflections of the armours of brave female warriors. Almost everywhere in Scandinavia, clear night skies are endearingly considered the harbinger of good news.

There is a lot to do but hearing all these stories entices us to make time for doing 'nothing' – staring at the sky, prying its myriad constellations, running fingers along snow-laden branches, gushing over perfectly-shaped snowflakes, taking in the sumptuous pin-drop silence in the woods and relishing the feeling of being just so far away from civilization.

On the last night, dinner is a creamy salmon soup, accompanied by a full-bodied red. We don't know whether it's the wine, exhaustion or sub-zero temperatures, but we're feeling heady as we tumble out of the restaurant.

We should sleep because we have an early-morning flight to catch. But the Arctic forest has other plans. It's a full-moon night and the entire snow-laden landscape is bathed in moonlight. Shadows play hide and seek as powdery snow continues to fall at a mellow pace. We crawl into the loungers in our igloo, wrap ourselves with blankets and prepare for another night of stargazing, and possibly spotting the Northern Lights. The snow continues to fall like little drops of confetti on the ceiling of our igloo – sometime around 3 a.m., exhaustion takes over and we doze off under a sky littered with tiny stars.

As two kids growing up in Delhi, we never understood why we could stare at airplanes all we wanted, but would never have enough money to go on an international vacation. Or why we had no option but to sleep without electricity on a sultry summer night.

Looking back, I think it was all for a reason – one neither of us understood then. As they say, *When you sleep in a house your aims are as high as the ceiling; when you sleep outside they are as high as the stars.*

This is the book of LIFE.

Part 1

Our Story

1

FAIRY TALES
Savi's Story

'*And then she wore that dress and played with the bears and rabbits all day long ...*

'Now go see if you brother wants any more food and come help me cook dinner – you'll cook chicken and tortillas for your family every week when you're older!'

I would've enquired which fairy tale that first sentence was from if her second statement hadn't thrown me off the way it did.

3

Sitting in a weaver's house in a little village by the shores of Lake Atitlan, the most scenic part of Guatemala, we were witness to the domestic rhythm of life. A number of slow travellers come to this bucolic corner of the world to hone their Spanish-speaking skills and the two of us were no different. We had come for a week, but three weeks later, we still hadn't left.

San Pedro isn't an easy place to get to. We took a flight to Guatemala City. Then a bus ride to Panajachel, the gateway to Lake Atitlan. Then a boat. As we clutched onto our bags on the local ferry and snaked our way towards a little village by Lake Atitlan, we could see why the area has been accorded such prominence in dozens of literary and geographical treatises. It truly is 'too pretty', if there is such a thing! A series of volcanic mountains frame a ring of azure water. Little villages, famous for colourful handicrafts and scrumptious food, are dotted around the entire perimeter of the lake. Traditional boats transport residents and tourists from one village to the other. Historical cathedrals and Mayan temples loom large, bright handicrafts adorn walls and hole-in-the-wall tortillerias beckon visitors. We lugged our suitcases uphill and reached our apartment, perched on top of a hillock in the village of San Pedro. Every morning we would get up and marvel at the view of Lake Atitlan. The lake, surrounded by indigenous villages and three stunning volcanoes, is truly one of a kind!

Inevitably we would head into town at midday, just in time to catch the local market. Ripe avocados being sold by the dozen; juicy passion fruit, bursting with flavour, by the kilo; freshly baked tostadas still warm from the oven; and crisp tostadas dipped in traditional black bean paste, frijoles negros, all the more impossible to resist due to the persistent calls of the vendors. San Pedro's local market spoilt our taste buds rotten. We'd never had avocados like that before – so creamy and velvety, they were almost sensual.

It was on one such midday roving that we first met her – sitting on the pavement with piles of bright red and pink scarves all around her. We stopped to pick one up – a distinctively Guatemalan souvenir for a friend. An animated spate of bargaining in our admittedly rotten Spanish, with frantic hand gestures, followed. Probably the best way to practice a new language.

With generous help from Google Translate. 'You have the warmest smile in the world – is it okay if I come to take a photograph of you tomorrow? Do you sit here every day?' Vid asked. Before we knew it, we had been invited to her house, in the neighbouring village, so that we could take a photograph of her weaving those scarves on a traditional loom. Of course, we said yes!

And here we were – sitting in her house, enraptured by the innocence of her little daughter's face! We had been there for over an hour but our camera was still in the bag.

Because the house was as most houses with young kids are – chaotic, messy and full of life. The superwoman in question was weaving, cooking a meal and reading a fairy tale to her daughter, all at once. It was a fairy tale I'd never heard before – about little girls building houses with the help of animals that talk.

The look of wonder in the girl's eyes reminded me of myself. I have loved books for as long as I can remember. My mom loved reading. And she ensured daily bedtime stories were an unsaid rule in our house. Every night after dinner, either my mom or dad would regale my brother and me with Noddy's adventures or fairy tales till we fell asleep. As a child, books were all that I ever wanted as presents. As a ten-year-old, with an early wake-up call, I would try finishing books with light from a torchlight under the blankets. Because I couldn't bear the thought of going to school the next day without having finished an interesting story. As a teenager, I would use all my pocket money to buy Nancy Drews, Secret Sevens, Agatha Christies and everything else out there. I didn't have any dolls or toys but I was very proud of the jam-packed bookshelf in my room.

Us humans, we love a good story. And books contain the ability to transport us to faraway lands, without so much as leaving the confines of our own rooms. Perhaps that's why we've been reading more than ever during the COVID-19 pandemic.

As I child, I would spend hours reading Enid Blyton and thinking of how things would be in the magic Faraway Land. Or what Alice would feel when she fell down the rabbit hole. I wanted to be at the Mad Hatter's tea party. I would imagine myself in topsy-turvy lands with kooky friends. As a quiet academic child, I used to live in a world entirely of my own.

I loved days off from school. Because they came with my favourite ritual of them all. My mother, a homemaker, would finish all her chores by midday and sit down to complete whatever book she had been reading. I've been told that as a toddler, I would sit next to her and try to imitate her by opening a magazine, when I couldn't read or write. But as I grew older, we would read together. And she would always make us a snack. So there we were, on a summer afternoon, reading our books and tucking into buttery popcorn.

'What if I don't want hair as long as Rapunzel,' I would ask her. 'It's a story, you can have it as short or as long as you'd like,' she'd tell me. 'Eww, I don't want to kiss a frog or find a prince,' I'd say. 'There's no rush. You don't have to find a prince if you don't want to.'

It would be 2 p.m. by the time our reading session would wind up and my father would come home from his clinic for lunch and a nap. We would always eat together as a family and questions continued at lunchtime. I wanted to believe the fairy tales but growing up in India,

I saw evidence to the contrary. Inequality, stemming from patriarchy, was all around us. Even as a child I heard disturbing tales at mealtimes. 'I get at least two pregnant women asking me to prescribe a gender-identification ultrasound each day. I refuse to do it. They'll kill it if it's a girl,' my dad would complain, battling the menace of female foeticide with exasperated sighs every day. I would hear about my aunt, whose husband flung plates at her when the food she cooked wasn't warm or tasty enough. About my mom's friend, who had a well-paying job but felt guilty about being unable to look after her kids. In a world saturated with inequality, who could make one believe in fairy tales?

Parents!

'I remember dancing and distributing chocolates in the whole hospital when I found out it was a girl,' my dad would say, smiling from ear to ear while going through photo albums. 'Your name is an amalgamation of both our names – Sa from Sangeeta and Vi from Ravi. That's how special you are. A part of each of us makes Savi.' 'Why don't both of you come sit with me in the kitchen as I bake this cake,' my mom would say to my brother and me, insisting we both clean up after. That was how both of us learnt to cook. Both of us learnt to do the laundry. That was how our home became a safe space devoid of any gendered stereotypes. A reassuring haven, in the midst of the madness.

I have to be honest. I grew up in that bubble. I did not understand the real worth of these lessons, imparted to us in matter-of-fact ways, mostly in passing, till I grew up. It was in high school and university that I began to grapple with the lopsided ways of patriarchy. And I was shocked at how it affected almost every girl and woman around me.

Studying English literature at university gave me a vocabulary to articulate my anger at this gender imbalance. My lifelong fascination with books came in handy. I wrote paper after paper deconstructing fairy tales, questioning the premise, the beginnings and the endings. I became passionate about teaching young girls, reassuring them in ways that their families had not – arming them with thoughts, words and dreams.

Perhaps that is why hearing the weaver woman prepare her daughter for the role of a caretaker, while pandering to her son's whims, took me for a walk down memory lane. We never did take a photo that day. The afternoon was spent devouring a scrumptious meal over a long conversation 'That's how things in Guatemala work. We need to prepare them for the future,' she explained. But I countered, 'The big bad world out there isn't a patch on what you learn at home. Parents that give their kids wings to fly, parents that don't clip wings based on gender are the best kind of parents. Teach your son and daughter to cook, teach him to help you around the house, teach her to dream. Trust me, I know!'

As we walked back to our apartment, I thought of the struggles women face on a daily basis all across the world just because of their gender. Of the things little girls and little boys internalize – the love for dolls or the colour pink, a false sense of machismo and the love for blue. Toys, clothes, strangers – they're all out to get us to fall into neat traps.

Equipping your kids to be good humans instead of men or women will lead to the real happy ending but sometimes it seems impossible. It's the twenty-first century but it's still as hard to equip your kids to approach the world with wonder in their eyes. 'The real world is such a killjoy,' I murmur as I thread my fingers through his.

Despite my parents' best efforts to give us a childhood free of inequality, I remember being confused by the reality of it all at the age of fifteen. One day after school, I jumped into my school bus, having heard the most heartbreaking story from my best friend. She was sexually assaulted by her uncle and when she finally gathered the guts to tell her parents, they dismissed it and pretended it never happened. After all, such tales could wreak havoc in families.

'I should've never told them but I was scared. What if it happens again?' she said, crying inconsolably and, at the time, I didn't know what to tell her. I was trembling as I sat down in the bus, still in shock.

10

Just then, on the seat behind me, I overheard a boy, 'I was helping my dad clean the house for guests, so I had to miss soccer practice.' I turned around. 'So geeky looking,' I thought. But then in the midst of the shock and the trembling, I smiled! When I heard him say that, I knew we were going to be friends, very good friends indeed. But even I did not know just what lay ahead!

2

BREAKING THE SHACKLES

Vid's Story

I remember meeting Savi for the first time at the back of a rickety school bus – a chubby girl with glasses trying to edge her way to the corner of a torn seat. I could tell something wasn't right. Was she in shock? Was she going to cry? Was it something serious?

I didn't know her. In fact, I had never seen her before but I saw the look on her face and I wanted to lend her an ear. But as an awkward teenager, I wasn't quite sure how! So I resorted to the only way I knew – cracking a lame joke, which no one found funny! I was a fumbling mess by the end of it but at least it made her smile.

We soon discovered we were neighbours and it was a matter of months before we were inseparable. I could speak to her for hours – she would talk about Enid Blyton books and secret wonderlands, and I would chuckle. 'Who is this girl? How has she made it this far? She needs to get back to the real world!'

I wasn't brought up on fairy tales. The only books I read growing up were comics or, worse still, text books that were prescribed in school. I was not given any incentives or treats to study. Like it was for most Indian kids, it was something that just had to be done. It was ingrained in our DNA. You need to sit for exams and come out with flying colours. Not doing well wasn't an option. So like clockwork, I would get home, have lunch, and study for hours at a stretch. If I had any free time, I'd slip out for a game of cricket with my friends in the colony. Exhausted after hours of playing in the heat of Delhi, the winning team would sometimes buy everyone 'chowmein' from the neighbourhood shack and we would enjoy our victory huddled over a plate of terribly spiced noodles while sitting on a stretch of pavement. Those were my outings … THAT was my childhood.

I saw my mom work hard to juggle work and family. I saw my father helping out my mom when she came back from work. I saw him cleaning and cooking when she was caught up with work. And as we grew up, my brother and I picked up those little things. We didn't have to be told. At age ten, we were like little adults, dressing ourselves up, studying when we were supposed to, playing when we were supposed to. All realism, no whims!

But as I pen this, I am sitting outside the most picturesque little cottage in Iceland. I can hear horses in the distance. It's -20°C outside, snowflakes are falling at a mellow pace and the sky is silvery. I've been nursing this cup of coffee for the past two hours and staring into the distance. I must confess I do this often. And Savi always asks me, 'What are you thinking of at this very moment.' And I always have the same answer, 'Nothing – I'm just giving my mind a break to take it all in, to truly enjoy the moment, the little things.' I'm in my thirties and, at last, I'm introducing my mind to fairy tales.

Perhaps that is why I have a deep-seated love affair with remote places. I can never get enough of them. And Iceland tops that list.

Three trips to the country later, I am convinced it is the proverbial pot of gold at the end of the rainbow. As we arrive at Reykjavik airport and settle into the seats of our SUV rental, I feel a strange sense of familiarity wash over me. This is where I'd been longing to be for over a year. I kick back and settle into the warm seat. All around me raging winds herald a snowstorm but strangely enough, I feel at home!

A couple of years ago, the two of us spent a languorous fortnight driving around Iceland. Splendid summer days and twenty hours of daylight ensured we spent our romantic getaway chasing waterfalls, sipping chilled beers outside scenic lodges, hiking to the tops of extinct volcanoes and unwinding in hot tubs in the middle of mountains. We tried to explore every nook and cranny we possibly could but Iceland refused to be relegated to the backburner as just a fond memory. Instead, it continued to call out to us over and over again. Many months of planning later, here we were, determined to get our teeth sunk into Iceland's winter landscapes.

We haven't yet left the airport but wailing winds and the sound of hailstones against our car force me out of this reverie, making me wonder whether I did the right thing convincing Savi to visit Iceland in the depth of winter! We cautiously snake our way out of the airport with a three-hour drive ahead of us. My heart is racing because I'm driving and I can't see a thing. It's only 2 p.m. but darkness is descending at a quick pace. There are several warnings for snowstorms on the radio.

Savi plugs in her USB stick and soon enough, the music system is belting out familiar ambient tunes. We continue driving, trying to underplay the apprehension by regaling each other with tales from our last trip. Over the next twenty minutes, as if by magic, the weather clears up. We see mountains looming ahead of us on the highway, lit only by the moonlight. As we marvel at the snow-capped peaks, I see a fleeting glimmer of something in the sky. It's gone even before I can figure out what it is. Five minutes later, I see a faint streak of green.

'It's the Northern Lights,' she whispers, as if the heavens would stop unleashing them if they heard us. 'Should we stop?' We pull up and step out of our car and there they are – magnificent aurora borealis colouring the sky green one moment and purple the next! We stand transfixed as we watch them dance, change colour, dart from one end of the sky to the other! She looks at me and smiles, because she knows exactly what I'm thinking – I'm so happy to be in Iceland.

Icelandic folklore has many stories about such sudden changes of weather that can be experienced in the country – you could go from wearing a T-shirt to a down jacket in the space of a single day. Witnessing this miracle unfold in front of our eyes, it is easy to see why even the most rational individuals would think this is the work of elves, working in tandem with fairies.

The next day, we sleep in. Sunrise is only at 10 a.m., which means winters in Iceland are perfect if your idea of a romantic getaway includes snuggling in bed for hours. At sunrise, we drive to the iconic Black Church of Budir. It might be small in structure but its signature black colour and the staggering views of the surrounding windswept landscape set the tone for the day. We hike to the Hellnar Arch, where limestone and basalt columns offer incredible views over volcanic moors. Here, naturally formed arches exist in unison with eerie phenomena like a pyramid-shaped volcano (Mt Stapafell!) and Snæfellsjökull glacier and volcano. As we admire the intricate limestone carvings along the way and sit down for a bowl of steaming hot fish soup and freshly baked bread, we chance upon several renditions of Bárður Snæfellsás (half troll, half man), also known as the Protector of the Snæfellsnes Peninsula. The restaurant owner entertains us with tales of the mythical Bárður, protecting Icelandic people from calamities in the region – just another example of the way folklore and nature come together to create magic in Iceland.

The next few days are spent driving to secret waterfalls in the area. We fawn over the mystical 'Lava Falls' where rivulets of flowing lava are punctuated with stalactites and stalagmites. I can't stop photographing rainbows stretched out over the iconic Gullfoss Waterfall. We stand awed by the surreal beauty of Kerid, a volcanic crater lake. We stare at frozen waterfalls. Iceland's waterfalls are gorgeous during all seasons but they seem otherworldly during winter months because dripping water frequently metamorphoses into icicles – time seems to come to a standstill here. And then there is Jokulsarlon Iceberg Lagoon. A lagoon full of floating icebergs, next to a black lava beach strewn with rocks of ice! How often do you hear all those words together in a sentence? We spend days walking by a beach dotted with hundreds of glistening rocks of ice that have been washed ashore. We go hiking on glaciers and camping in secret caves that are formed under glaciers each year. These blue caves are barely illuminated but endlessly fascinating. An icy wonderland carved entirely by Mother Nature. There's a whole world down there and we find ourselves smitten!

Some nights, we huddle in our warm car and watch the Northern Lights over Mount Kirkjufell – the distinctively shaped mountain, next to a cascading waterfall, that can be spotted in many postcards of Iceland. As I watch star-spangled skies coloured green, purple and pink, I can't help but wonder if this is where the mythological creatures come to play. It is freezing but I spend entire nights outside just looking at the dance of the Northern Lights. At the northern tip of Iceland, they're green one moment, purple the next. After an hour of hunting for the mighty aurora borealis, Savi will often rush back to our cottage for a cup of hot chocolate. But me? I'll be relishing the Northern

Lights as my camera makes time-lapse videos of the magic. Iceland's wilderness speaks to me.

Every conversation with locals is packed with references to tiny little houses carved for *huldufólk* (mythical hidden people) or an odd rock in a lava field that is said to be an 'elf church'. I don't know if it is Icelandic folklore or its incredible scenery, but Iceland's wilderness makes even the avid realist in me believe in fairy tales!

But fairy tales of our own making. I remember snippets of a conversation during a game of truth and dare in the school bus. 'What would you do if you won a lottery?' she asked me. I looked down at my atlas; thought of the threat of the upcoming semester exams looming over my head and perhaps that was why I muttered, 'Travel the world, with no worries at all.' Little did I know what lay ahead.

It took both Savi and me over a dozen years of planning and working to be able to realize our dream of travelling full time. As teenagers, we took up odd jobs – everything from teaching English to international students to tutoring high-school students to invigilating – to pay our university fees. Once we started earning, we would try to travel as much as we could whilst saving for full-time travel on the side.

As our friends were buying jewellery and houses, we were saving for a life of full-time travel. But the challenges were not just financial in nature. Choosing an unconventional life meant our choices were constantly questioned by friends, family, and even random strangers! Reactions would range from curiosity to dislike to ideological battles.

In fact, after almost twelve years of saving and working towards a fund that would enable us to travel full-time, there came a time when both of us were almost discouraged from pursuing our dreams. Till one day, a random conversation with my dad after Savi and I had completed a seventy-kilometre-long hike in Australia, convinced me. He said, 'Congratulations! I wish I had done these things when I still had the chance. Now I'm seventy and I have the time, but lack the energy.' Weirdly, his momentary regret made me decide to pursue my craziest dream. We had been mulling over our decision to quit our day jobs and travel full-time for weeks. But that night I told Savi, 'Let's do it.'

I thought about that crazy leap of faith as we shared a fleeting afternoon with three Masai tribesmen in Zanzibar, a little island off the coast of Tanzania. I think the ice was broken when I asked them their 'real' names, not the ones English-speaking tourists find easy to pronounce! The five of us were the only ones at a lone beach on a quiet summer afternoon – the two of us being curious travellers, venturing to little corners nobody ever writes about; the

Masai tribesmen were just catching a nap under the shade. I waved to them. 'Honeymoon?' one of them said, pointing to us. 'We've been married for ages,' I said with a smile. One thing led to another, till we were conversing about life, love and everything in between in broken English and hand gestures. We spoke about tourism and what it has done to the island, daily life in Tanzania, and I asked a lot of inane questions about Tanzanian food! We bonded over being unable to understand the fascination with selfies. At the end of the afternoon, we had to leave. They 'blessed' us with an ancient guiding proverb of the Masai, *Happiness nourishes you as much as food.*

While that might be true, we humans love tangible returns. In fact, one of the questions I'm asked almost on a daily basis by curious friends, inquisitive colleagues, disapproving family members and everyone in between! 'What's your ultimate dream?' I think they expect me to respond with, 'My dream is to travel to every country in the world.' Perhaps that I'd love to be on a magazine cover. But to be honest, none of those are it! My only dream is to live a life that makes us happy and content each day. I get to spend my days pursuing my passion with an amazing woman I love, so I'm already living my dream each day of my life. *Happiness nourishes you as much as food.*

I can say this today, but not long ago, we were just two kids, unsure of the future, with wonder in our eyes and our entire life packed into a bag each. Free of shackles.

22

Ready to see what the world had to offer. It took time, but we managed to shut out the outside noise, take that leap of faith and quit our jobs. But would we miss the familiarity of home? Would we be able to make this sustainable and earn an income on the go? Would we get homesick? I won't lie – we were excited, we were scared and we were nervous. But here's what I told myself – wherever life took us, we were in this together.

3

FINDING HOME

I look through the ivory mosquito net, sunlight streaming through glass windows, the fragrance of fresh rain wafting in through the netting. Mornings like this make me smile from ear to ear.

Vid is still fast asleep, but I gather the bedspread and wrap it around myself. It's been raining all night – there's a nip in the air and the countryside is alight with neon greenery. As I sit in our patio, nursing my morning coffee, I can hear the distant crowing of roosters and bells tinkling at the neighbourhood temple. I sink in deeper into my bamboo chair, relishing the early-morning calm. Ubud – she's a little bit of heaven with a wild side! Fluidity is the word that best describes the months we spend here – days flow into each other, hours swim into one another – languorous massages, working to the sound of rain and falling leaves against the windows, bike rides along dusty alleys and sumptuous organic meals. We become one with the curtains dancing around our room. We swivel and feel like we're drifting into our version of utopia, with eyes half closed. Ubud, it feels like homecoming.

I close my eyes as I think about how I feel at home here – in a little village in Bali, surrounded by paddy fields on all sides. Growing up, we were always taught home is a place. I remember sitting at a rickety desk in school, writing an essay on 'Home' as a ten-year-old with the help of a compact book of essays, formulated specially for an academic system that promoted rote learning. Long essays were punctuated with sentences highlighted in red, 'Home is a safe place, a place you come to after work. One day I will buy my own house and make it a home with love and care.' Looking back, it was crammed full of platitudes, one after the other. A quick learner, I would reel them off, much to the delight of my parents and teachers. Years later, I learnt that these phrases were not purely superficial

– they were drilled into the collective psyche of entire societies.

Despite living in a bustling metropolis, growing up in professional households in India during the eighties and nineties meant we were continuously subject to a steady stream of bourgeois rhetoric. All around us, pop culture percolated down at a lag. Movies were aired in cinema halls months after their international release. Trends made their way to India long after they had gone out of fashion in the West. Smartphones didn't exist. And pen pals were still a thing! We would buy dictionaries and encyclopaedias to acquire information in the comfort of our rooms. Access to any sort of counter-culture was already severely limited due to technology. But overzealous parents would go a step further and prohibit it altogether.

I remember the time one of my dad's friends became an Osho devotee and decided to move from Delhi to a little village in Goa. All of us went to bid goodbye to him. On our way back, squeezed between my uncle and aunt in the backseat of our trusty white Maruti 800, I heard alternative lifestyles being dismissed as 'hippie', 'not sustainable', 'immature'.

'They'll grow out of it and change their tune.' We heard that line a lot. And change they did. The occasional outlier we saw while growing up, eventually toed the bourgeois line of thought. That's because all of us were taught to think of life as a checklist – you grow up, you educate yourself as much as you possibly can, get a stable job, get married, have kids and build a home for yourself. The template of a successful life.

To everybody around me – relatives, uncles, aunts and cousins – home was the culmination of his or her achievements in life. Your entire being was judged by the kind of neighbourhood you resided in. Could you afford luxurious furnishings or would you wrap your television remotes in plastic? Whether your house had two bedrooms or four? Bricks and mortar – responsible for evaluating the entire worth of people's lives. Imagine that!

'But what about savouring life?' he murmured as we negotiated puddles in Bali's flooded bylanes on our brightly coloured Vespa. Bit by bit we are trying to unlearn things that have been fed to us at school, university, and in the corporate world. We spend a few hours working on our computers while sipping on tender coconut water. We discover a village, not found in any guidebook, while picking up our host's son from primary school. We drive through paddy fields and go hunting for tiny waterfalls.

We learnt as we went along – as we started to take little steps towards cultivating happiness and contentment in our lives, that things that used to bother us, didn't anymore. We learnt lessons that aren't ever taught at school – prioritize happiness, prioritize contentment and those people in your life who love you as much as you love them. While my competitive self struggles with practising contentment in order to relish the present, that last dictum comes easily to me. In fact, since I can remember, my little nuclear family has meant everything to me. Till an unforeseen event changed my family forever.

Growing up, like most people, I thought heartbreaks, failed fitness goals, etc., were enough to get me down in the dumps! Then I lost my dad to a stroke out of the blue. He was also my best friend, confidant and the one who taught me to live life on my own terms, and give back to society in any way I could! He was a doctor and the healthiest person I knew and, just like that, he was gone! That is when I knew what it felt like to be low. To feel physically maimed! To have my heart wrung out of my body! I thought it would get better. It did not.

For six months I didn't leave my apartment or talk to anyone. For three years after that, I couldn't get myself to tell anyone or even talk about it, except a handful of people close to me. In fact, if I didn't have the best friends and family to pull me out of that phase, I fear I would've descended deeper and deeper into that darkness. It's been eight years now. They say time heals but they lie! You crumble every single day and just learn to live with wounds that deep! Every time I see the crashing waves, Northern Lights or carpets of stars, I can actually feel my dad egging me on to new adventures and telling me not to cry because he's right there with me. 'Dad it's happening, I'm going on lots of new adventures,' I tell him. 'Thank you for equipping me with the will to rebel and fight stereotypes.' Then I cry – every single time! I could never obey him a 100 per cent. Love doesn't always have a happy ending and grief is so hard to accept. It paralyses you and hurts every single day. But I've learnt to hang in there. And you might not be better off for it, but you'll be stronger. Let the grief empower you in little ways. And empower it does.

Every time I would visit Delhi between travels, I would feel guilty for complaining about the sensory overload that awaited me the second I stepped off the plane. You could call it a ritual. Upon exiting the airport, we would wrestle our way to the pre-paid taxi booth. There we would spy officials conning customers with a sleight of hand if they looked at their phone or their companions even for a split second – they would throw the Rs 500 note handed to them on the floor and replace it with a Rs 100 note and ask the customer for the remaining fare amount with a straight face. The big-city circus. Well warned, we would hold on tight to the currency in our hands and wait for our turn.

Minutes later, as we elbowed our way to a queue of distinctive yellow and black cabs, I would find myself wishing to escape the sights and sounds. I would want to hop on a bus and head to the little villages of the Himalayas. This need to escape the city for a slower rhythm of life relentlessly nags us. But we question ourselves. We grew up here, we can handle it. I feel guilty about complaining because nobody understands. I feel so guilty that I would rather overdose on my asthma medications and pretend to be fine than admit Delhi's pollution was bothering me. It is no secret. When you've heard something repeatedly while growing up, it acquires the status of a 'fact'. Perhaps endless iterations by parents, teachers, society and friends had ensured the idea of home as a place was lodged somewhere at the back of my mind?

This went on for years. The guilt. But soon after my dad passed away, something changed. I remember going on a long drive in Delhi and staring glassy-eyed at familiar landmarks – India Gate, Rajpath, Connaught Place. I had so many memories at each of these places – looking forward to Sundays because it meant driving to India Gate to get ice creams from the dozens of colourful carts lining the roundabout. Bargaining for clothes and jewellery with college friends at Janpath. Skipping breakfast to have pastries and kebabs at Wenger's. Making an occasion out of going to see Rashtrapati Bhavan, all lit up on Republic Day.

But for a few years now, all I see are hospital wards. 'You can say your goodbyes,' they told us. I clutched onto his hand till all the warmth left his body, stroking his arm till it started to turned cold and stiff. 'Don't go, don't go, please don't go – we still need to go to Brazil together,' I whispered urgently, reminding him of his unfulfilled dream, even though I knew he couldn't hear a thing in his coma. It was something I'd heard him say since I was a little girl – he had watched a documentary on a videotape in the eighties and decided he'd visit Rio once in his life. We heard that story many times but he never made it there. Let's just say life got in the way. He worked seven days a week for his entire life till we grew up and forced him to go on little holidays. Even so, he didn't have much by way of savings because he put his entire life's earnings into buying a modest house for all of us. A family home that means nothing now! Because I want him, not the house! Bricks and mortar, more meaningless now than ever. We're driving in Delhi. But since his passing, all I can see are visions of my dad, fading in and out. Everywhere I look.

Perhaps it was at a moment like this that the guilt vanished. It was replaced by a strange sense of calm acceptance. These landmarks, which defined my childhood, did not define me anymore. I would love to have a little nest in Delhi to stay close to my family between travels. I would also love to have little homes in my favourite cities like Bali and London someday (a girl can dream!).

But I would never look at the concept of home the same way again. I realized the idea of home that had been fed to us did not mean anything to me. Because I could not let a building be the focal point of our achievements or attachments. It would never be the be-all and end-all of our existence. Both of us could accord such importance only to people or experiences in our lives.

The city where I grew up in is often not the place I crave for. I crave the palms, I crave a cottage in the snow, I crave walks by the beach, I crave fiery sunsets. I crave the slow rhythm of places. I had known that for a long time. But suddenly that was okay. Sometimes it takes a monumental loss to come to a point where you are finally ready to cut the umbilical cord. That night I came to terms with my definition of home, one that wasn't handed down to me. One that I had chosen for myself.

With pieces of my heart in Delhi, London and Bali, with nowhere to call home now, I felt at home in the world. New places invigorate me. Meeting people and exchanging tales excite me. It's an inexplicable rush and one thing's for sure – unlike the outliers I met as a kid, I'm not going to grow out of it!

I've come to accept I will never associate buildings or cities with 'forever' but some things will always be home – friends' hugs, mom's food, coming back to Vid's familiar kisses at the end of a long day, a starlit sky. That's home. Home for me is not a place but a feeling. People. Sensations. Moments. The road. Home is amorphous. But always, deeply comforting.

Travelling has taught me to think of home as a fluid concept. To some people it means saving up to buy a bungalow. To others, it means stability attached to a piece of land. But to us, it is simply the feeling of belonging in many different places across the globe. Living a peaceful life and, more importantly, a truly happy life in corners of the Earth that feel like a warm embrace. Corners where we've left parts of our soul. That school in Rajasthan, where we taught little kids. That cafe in Cusco where we met a musician with the most spell-binding voice ever. The balcony in Bali. That cottage in Iceland. The shack by the beach in Vietnam. These are the homes that make us feel truly rich! Like we have aced the checklist of life. In a way entirely our own.

And I like to think this happened because we were not scared to think BEYOND! Beyond the roles society laid out for us. Beyond the dreams others had for us. Beyond the expectations of strangers. Beyond the home we were told to have. We were not scared to imagine a future that made us smile every single day beyond the shackles of gender, circumstance or stereotypes.

Of course, being constantly on the go comes with its downsides. Missing home-cooked food on a cold day. Being unable to attend a childhood friend's birthday party. Missing the birth of a niece. But even for those who had a permanent address, to whom 'home' was a place they'd grown up and spent their life, home wasn't always the most comfortable place in the world, as we were about to find out …

4

PERSPECTIVE

'It's a glaze over the eyes, a crisis of not feeling,' she said as she poured some more orange juice into my glass.

'I could've never imagined a teenager in Denmark would feel like that. To my teenage self their life was THE life,' I muttered in response, still trying to process the conversation.

Sunlight streamed through the glass walls of the greenhouse, lighting up our breakfast table. We were in a rented apartment on the outskirts of Copenhagen and our hosts, a young Dane married to a Turkish man, had graciously asked us to join them for Sunday breakfast at their house.

Breakfast started innocently enough at 9 a.m. She taught us how to make smørrebrød (open sandwiches) with local ingredients – buttered rye bread, pickles, egg salad, paté, crunchy slivers of radishes and onions, and a sprig or two of fresh herbs. We exchanged travel tales and spoke about the magic of the Northern Lights. About driving along the Aegean coast in Turkey. About their first time in India and the sensory overload that followed.

This might be the first time we're having this conversation with her but it's a conversation we've had before – with AirBnB owners in Cusco, with a lone hiker in New Zealand, with a digital entrepreneur in Bali. I recognize the rhythm of this conversation. We hop between continents and exchange experiences as we tuck into a scrumptious meal. Soon enough, it's time to say goodbye.

I mention an article I recently read about *fika*, the Scandinavian custom of taking the time to enjoy a coffee and pastry with a friend. We talk about just how besotted the world is with everything Scandinavian at the minute – minimalism, open sandwiches, Vikings. Then, of course, there is fika, often touted as the key to happiness and contentment in a fast-paced world.

Perhaps that's when things changed for her. Like us, this was familiar terrain for them too. They hosted new travellers in their apartment every week. They were used to conversations that would hop between dozens of countries while sitting around a rustic table in Copenhagen. 'Things are not always how they seem – there is so much more to it,' she said. I looked at her and instantly knew that we were all in unfamiliar territory now. Rudimentary travel tales had been exchanged, breakfast had been devoured, it was time to say goodbye. Except in this case, the four of us were firmly glued to our seats, for the real conversation was only just starting. We might have been running out of coffee on that table, but we had all the time in the world.

Intrigued, both of us looked at her. 'Scandinavia is one of the happiest places on Earth. It offers its residents a really high standard of living. I hear this often. And it is. But there is so much more to it. Growing up in the countryside, we had access to everything – I had a comfortable house, I had food on the table, and I went to a great school. I got swimming lessons in the neighbourhood. I told my parents I wanted to learn the piano and soon enough I had one. All my classmates were like me too. But three of my friends committed suicide before they turned eighteen. I'm thirty now. Clinical anxiety and depression were everywhere and a lot of us felt like we had no purpose in life. Back then, my friends and I felt alienated from the world around us.

"Why me?" I would question the heavens. I would sneak into the moors with my friends and spend hours there.

'But now I know, we weren't alone. In fact, I see people like that at work every single day. They need to be informed about an evening social or barbecue at least ten weeks in advance. They come to work and leave exactly at 5 p.m. every day. To others, that is because our work–life balance is the best in the world. But I can see it for what it is. Robotic. It's a glaze over the eyes, a crisis of not feeling. The hunger is missing. In fact, it was his hunger for doing well at work that made me fall in love with Esin in the first place,' she smiled while signalling for her husband to top up the coffee!

'I could've never imagined a teenager in Denmark would feel like that. They had access to the music I wanted to listen to, they weren't pressurized to be academically successful, they could wear whatever they wanted, they could even date, without ever once getting scolded by teachers or parents. To my fifteen-year-old self, their life was THE life,' I told Vid that evening, still trying to process the conversation, all the while googling the suicide statistics of Nordic countries. It was her use of the word 'hunger' that continued to nag me. I always believed it was our hunger to chart our own story that got us here. Hunger to look beyond our circumstances. Hunger to look beyond what society expected of us.

But that morning's conversation had made me look at our hunger in a different light. A whole new perspective! Would it have been the same if we had everything? Can comfort handicap you? These were the questions that lulled me to sleep that day.

Perspective! It's a word that stayed with us long after this conversation in 2012. When we first started travelling, I would often curse my Indian passport because I needed a visa for every single country. This meant filling endless forms, compiling documents, reserving hotels and buying air tickets even before applying for the visas – it was a process I detested. I wanted flexibility. I wanted to travel the world. But diplomatic technicalities held me back – a quagmire of paperwork, agony and, oftentimes, wastage, when travel plans went to nought because visas didn't arrive in time. It held me back.

This narrative fed well into the angst of my friends who grew up in Delhi – we would gossip about limited opportunities for the arts in the developing world or how widespread sexism in India made it hard for women to make a mark. I would keep up the tone of this conversation by regaling my friends with tales of that time I lost Rs 100,000 of my hard-earned money just because my visa didn't come on time, or how much I resent the German Embassy for making me miss out on the opportunity of a lifetime to visit ten new countries during an exchange programme.

But as we continued to travel the world, things began to change. What happened in Copenhagen wasn't a solitary incident. I heard many such stories. Some days, they were about growing up in the first world. On others, they were about living in the lap of nature in Uganda or relishing life on a ranch in Brazil. It was on one such morning, my mind swimming with stories, that we landed in Addis Ababa with some friends from London.

I'll be honest. Addis Ababa is a city that throws you off. There is precious little about it online and the scramble for taxis, ATMs and guides smacks you in the face almost as soon as you leave the airport. We bundle ourselves into a cab and reach our hotel. It's past midnight, so venturing into the city isn't an option. Most of our friends fall asleep, while the two of us, curious as ever, tiptoe into a neighbouring hole-in-the-wall eatery looking for a snack. 'No snacks, we close the kitchen at midnight,' says the lanky teenager, sitting in the corner, glued to his phone.

I turn to walk to the hotel but Vid's made his way to the other side of the serving station. 'You might want to tone down the shadows,' I hear Vid say. I had assumed the teenager was playing games on his phone, but it takes one photographer to know another. Soon enough, Vid is teaching him some of his favourite editing tricks on the Lightroom app and asking him about his favourite photography spots in Addis Ababa. Before we know it,

Aron is inviting us to his place for a meal, because it is his cousin's birthday party.

My growling tummy says yes but I can sense the apprehension in Vid's eyes too. It's almost 1 a.m. We're in a new country with a stranger we've barely exchanged a few conversations with! But we decide to throw caution to the wind and take a leap of faith. A fifteen-minute walk leads us to a modest home, packed with elders, couples and teenagers. Loud music is punctuated by a baby's wails. The walls are bedecked with birthday decorations and I spy the remains of a cake lying listlessly on the table.

We have nothing for the birthday boy, so hugs will have to do. Aron and his sister take us to the kitchen, where something smells amazing! Ethiopian food is a firm favourite of ours, so I can't wait to see how home-cooked Ethiopian food compares to what we've had in restaurants in other countries. A huge plate is precariously balanced on a makeshift table, surrounded by four stools. A spongy flatbread, injera, is placed on the plate and our hosts top it up with the remnants of a feast – small portions of stews from almost a dozen different pots and pans. Before we begin eating, Aron rounds off a bit of the injera and feeds it to Vid with his hands. '*Gursha*,' he points to the bite. This intimate gesture is a way of Ethiopians to make their guests feel welcome. Everyone eats from the same plate in Ethiopia, so for the next half an hour, there is precious

41

little conversation. Just four adults hunched over a massive plate of food. Aron is tired and hungry after his long shift at the restaurant – his sister waited for him to get home so she could give him company. As for us, we're famished after the long day. We sample everything from doro wat (chicken stew) to some leftover shiro (chickpea paste) but his mom's misir wat (spicy red lentils) and tomato salad are my favourites. We wrap up the meal with tej, a local mead made from unprocessed honey and gesho, a species of buckthorn. We've had a lot of these dishes before, but here in the cramped kitchen of an Ethiopian household, they taste better! Spices, garnishes and the ambience come together to create culinary magic that is hard to find while travelling the world with a checklist in hand.

The next morning is no different – we reel off our adventures to our friends as we cross fashionable cafes next to slums, shanty towns in scenic locations, upscale restaurants flanked by beggars, often little kids pretending to be handicapped. It was there – standing at the crossroads in Addis Ababa, waiting for the signal to turn green for pedestrians – that it struck me.

We are in a new country, one we haven't ever been to. We are with a group of well-travelled people. They're all taken aback by the unique fabric of Addis Ababa. But we feel strangely confident. We're happy to navigate the alleyways of the city alone. We know the little kids might be persistent in asking for spare change, but they are purely creatures of circumstance. Our first impulse is to mourn their lost childhood instead of getting annoyed at them. Suddenly, childhood in a developing country seems like an asset, one that makes us feel comfortable even in those corners of the world that throw off the most seasoned of travellers.

And this isn't the first time and it won't be the last. I remember stepping into a rickety rental car in Tunisia. The smidgeon of doubt that crept upon us on seeing the torn seats of the car and the paper on which the manager of the car-rental booth insisted on writing our credit card details, right down to the last digit. The instinctive trust we felt, when he responded to our grievances, by pointing to an Apple sticker on his battered car, insisting the car in question was as premium as an Apple device, no less!

Or the way the face of our Bedouin guide in Jordan lit up when we said yes to his rather odd suggestion, of going off the marked path in the Wadi Rum Desert so that we could catch a better sunset. Hours later, as we sat huddled around a fire, he would tell us how he had smiled from ear to ear when we agreed because most guests say no to this 'crazy' suggestion! Tunisia. Jordan. Ethiopia – travelling in the developing world is a learning curve, but we grew up in India, so we come equipped!

As we prepare for the flight out of Addis Ababa, I hand over my passport to the immigration official. A whirlpool of thoughts cloud my mind as I wait for him to put yet another stamp on the battered booklet. We grew up disliking our passports but was the Indian passport really a handicap? Didn't it just empower me to make new friends and have dinner at someone's house? Or explore a foreign country without a care in the world? Didn't it help me navigate the streets that seemed intimidating to everyone else in our group?

It was this empowering diversity that brought Ella and Alexander (names changed to protect privacy) to India. In our pledge to experience everything life had to offer, we had enrolled ourselves in what can only be described as a wellness sanctuary for bohemian souls – a tantra retreat in the Himalayas. That's where we met them.

As we lay sprawled under a tree after intense bodywork, I overheard Alexander telling our yoga teacher, 'Ella and I have spent the last five months living in a Rs 150 per night room by the Ganges in Rishikesh. Some days it would be flooded and the door wouldn't close. We've been knee-deep in muck too. But it's a lot better than being back home. I was spiralling in Denmark – I just wanted to test my body instead of getting caught in the cycle of depression. No one gets it!' he said. There would've been a time when I would've dismissed him in seconds. 'It's his privilege talking,' I would've said. After all, I had spent years romanticizing the Scandinavian way of life as the ideal. But sitting there, under the heady influence of music and tantric exercises, my mind darted to that conversation in Copenhagen and the way in which life has unfolded since. 'I get it, more than you know!' I murmured as they continued their conversation oblivious to my eavesdropping.

The world is a puzzle. It throws dots at us. Dots that perplexed us for years. For us those dots finally began to connect as we inched closer to thirty. Gradually, I stopped grumbling – perhaps because I had a newfound respect for roots. Roots that made me who I am. Fissures are a part of every society. It's how you deal with those obstacles that decide the course of your life! Perspective! People often ask us why we never grumble. Or how we see the glass as half-full instead of half-empty. Perspective!

They say travel is the greatest teacher of them all! It taught us something no textbooks ever could – it taught us to look at the ways in which gender, circumstance and nationality empower us instead of crippling us. Perhaps that's why they say, travel feeds the soul.

5

CELEBRATE

That's how we got the courage to embrace the world with open arms, without fears or worries. The seductive rhythm of travelling persuaded us that there are friends waiting to be made everywhere. It taught us to be proud of our roots. It led us to dismiss stereotypes. It encouraged us to trust our intuition more. Perhaps it was travel that taught us to be at peace with ourselves?

I think of this as I stare at wondrous rock formations in the Khizi District of Azerbaijan. We're in the middle of a road, flanked by mountains on both sides. But they are no ordinary mountains. They're covered, from the precipice to the foothills, in swirls that remind me of red and white candy canes one minute and pale-pink strawberry ice cream with bits of cherries the next. There is no one as far as the eye can see.

'Let's go on a hike?' I ask. The words have barely left my lips when I smile. It's a rhetorical question, of course – I know he's going to say yes. I feel most travellers go through a rite of passage – all of us start off scared of the world that awaits us. But once it starts unveiling its wonders, we find ourselves falling in love with it. Then there comes a stage where a mix of heartwarming and ugly encounters leave us unsure. This is also the juncture when some of us give up! 'It rained the entire time I was there' or 'My wallet was stolen on the train' is often followed by 'Urgh! I'm done exploring the world!'

But if you're stubborn, then you take those little episodes in your stride. 'Yes it rained, but look at all the conversations I had while we huddled around the fire with warm brandy! And all those new friends I made?' a little voice tells you at the back of your mind. You begin to realize those little setbacks are just Mother Nature's way of telling you nothing is ever perfect. Perhaps it is at this point you realize you've fallen irrevocably in love with the world, faults and all. And once you're there, there's no going back. The world reveals surprise after surprise and you can't help but celebrate them endlessly.

This feeling of freedom in the Azeri hinterland just cannot be compared to anything else in the world. We're squinting in the sun as beads of sweat trickle down our backs, but we carry on. Soon, we're at the top of the hill surrounded by candy-cane mountains on all sides, our car just a little speck in the distance. I can't shake off the heady feeling as we walk back to the car and drive deeper into the Azeri countryside, excited about what lies ahead.

Soon enough, paved roads give way to steep cliffs and gravel paths with steep drops. We spot stray horse riders and goat herders as we make our way to the northernmost village of Europe – Xinaliq. As the sun sets, it feels like we've stepped back in time. And just then, a flat tyre!

Somewhere in the greater Caucasus, close to the Russian border. No petrol pumps. No shops. Heck, no people. Just a flat tyre and us. We regret not having checked the condition of the spare tyre while renting the car. Sometimes you don't have an option but to wait! We nibble on apples and a lone bag of popcorn hoping someone will come along to help us. Forty minutes later, a passer-by. An elderly gentleman, as luck would have it.

Had our wild hand gestures conveyed our desperation? Could we get help? I wonder as he points to something around the nearest bend, before resuming his evening stroll. Unwilling to leave our passports and luggage in the car, we put on extra woollens and start pushing the car towards the bend. A scraped hand and a squashed foot later, we see twinkling lights and a village of some sort. Just a handful of houses. So that was what he was pointing towards.

'We're doomed!' I whisper. 'What now?' The euphoria of the morning hike was dying a slow death. Feeling thoroughly spent, I don't even know what to hope for. But before we can look for anyone, a bunch of curious kids come up to us. 'Do you need help?' tentative English with a distinctively British accent. Was I imagining things? Peppa Pig, Peppa Pig – the other kids teased the little boy! At that moment, I loved nothing more than kids' cartoons. We had finally found someone who could guide us in the right direction. We frantically try to ask him the name of the village, explain our situation, quiz him about the surroundings. He nods as if he understands everything, mutters something about dinner and then just wanders off, probably bored of being questioned by two frazzled adults. 'No, no, don't go, you were supposed to be our salvation,' I want to say! For the first time in a long time, I want to cry while travelling.

Just then, I feel a tiny hand clutch me by the wrist. Before we know it, a little girl, perhaps five years old, is dragging us to her house – a modest space with a tin roof. It's dinnertime. We walk in and try to explain our

situation to the adults of the family. After much to and
fro, we realize most homes in the area double up as local
homestays during summer months. They have no guests,
so their spare room is ours for the taking! We make a little
trip to our car for essentials as her mother makes fragrant
fresh kutabs – flatbreads stuffed with spinach. The rest of
the evening goes by in a blur – the adults dispersed after
dinner but the little girl – Fatima – clung to us like a little
lamb. She didn't talk much but she spent the entire evening
sitting on my lap playing games on an old cellular phone.

Everything that could go wrong had gone wrong
that day. At another time it would've made me swear off
travelling – it's a good thing we're among the stubborn
ones! That night, as we snuck into bed in what seemed
like a forgotten land, I scribbled something in my tattered
travel journal in the dim candlelight:

'You can't travel like that on an Indian passport,' they
said.

But my eyes lit up just at the thought of snow-clad
villages that I'd never seen till then!

'How will you ever save enough to travel full-time?
There's no one to help you out if your savings run out!'
they said.

But my brain was already fantasizing about
spending months in a little village in Tuscany!

'How can you take the risk of quitting the jobs you've studied for?' they said.

But I could already feel the rush of seeing zebras and penguins in the wild in Africa!

'What if you get unwell on the road? What if you get bored of living out of suitcases? What if you miss home comforts? What if? What if? What IF?' they said.

But I didn't want to have a single regret when I turned seventy.

the tranquility after
hike through the
rests of Canada.

Alberta, Canada, is a must for your bucket list.

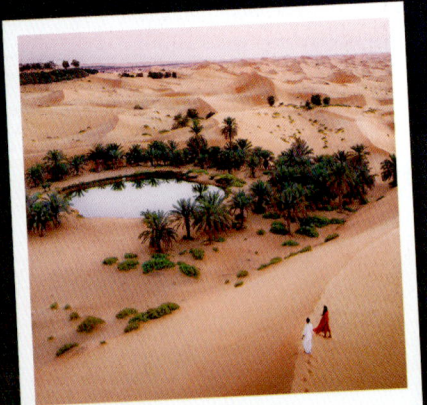

Don't forget to visit an oasis when in Abu Dhabi.

We loved the famous
Sheikh Zayed Grand
Mosque in Abu Dhabi.

Experience nature
its primal best at th
Arctic Circ

Beautiful snow-capped trees at Lake Blausee in Switzerland.

Switzerland is on everyone's list! How we loved roaming about the streets of Zurich.

Give Slovenia a try for your next winter holiday.

With its cherry blossom
trees and snowy mountains,
both of us loved Japan.

Some countries lend themselves to a roadtrip – like New Zealand – but India has many such scenic routes too!

Always have some hot chai at a roadside dhaba in Ladakh.

We had to add our own twist to a photo by the Pangong Lake in Ladakh.

Australia, the land down under
is full of charms. Th
is us soaking in Brisban

Welcome
Savi &
Vidit
*Bruised
Passports

Nothing beats the great
Australian coast, and
what better way to enjoy
it than to drive around!

Always immerse yourself in local
culture – like I did in Peru!

Bali will always have our heart, from beautiful structures like the Handara Gate to the natural beauty, the country is breathtaking.

Travel tip: dress in layers for your trip!

As I say later: the earth
is alive in Iceland.

Montenegro

Romancing in Italy

With Masai Mara tribesmen
in Tanzania

For an off-the-beaten-path
trip, head to Lapland.

We love a good vantage point –
like this one in Montenegro.

Oman, the land of the sparkling sea and sprawling wadis.

Shillim has emerged as a hot favourite
in Maharashtra these recent years.

herever you go,
ways try and
scover hidden
ms for memories
at will last forever.

Part 2

Trips to last a lifetime

6

20 ICONIC BUCKET-LIST ADVENTURES

They deem me mad because I will not sell my days for gold; and I deem them mad because they think my days have a price.

I remember this quote by Kahlil Gibran scribbled on a 'travellers wall' at a nondescript eatery in Siem Reap but it has stayed with me through the years.

People assume I travelled a lot as a child, which led me to exploring the world as an adult. But the truth is, I did not step foot on a plane till I was almost eighteen!

Growing up, my dad (a doctor) and my mom (a homemaker) spent all their earnings to provide the best possible education and standard of living to my brother and me. So holidays were few and far between. But when I stepped on the first flight, I remember marvelling at the sheer splendour and wizardry of aircrafts. A stretch of turbulence left the most seasoned travellers in the flight flummoxed, but I was grinning all throughout. Is that how you know you love something? When you accept it, as it is, drawbacks, turbulence and all?

I don't know about others, but for me that was the start of a passionate love story. And this is why in the age of arm-chair travelling, when you can experience the entire world by just scrolling through your Instagram feed, I recommend the real thing to everyone!

Why should one get off that chair and go travelling? There is nothing you can't find on the mighty internet! From countless inspirational photos to detailed itineraries, everything is available at the tap of a finger. The sheer amount of information means we spend innumerable hours poring over potential itineraries. Social media can seduce you with photos and lure you into dreaming of faraway destinations.

The greatest irony is that this sheer mass of information that is meant to coax people into travelling the world has actually made voyeurs of us all. We click on adventure after adventure whilst sipping on our morning tea, read regaling tales of exotic cities on our laptops and peruse endless photos of picturesque locations – all from the confines of tiny cubicles in our respective offices. Those cubicles are our safety net, if you may!

But here's the thing – reading about somebody else's travels is all well and good but there's a special quality about travelling that even the most articulate travel writer can't put into words – I like to call it the SMELL of travel.

That's because it is hard to explain how the lingering warmth of buttery popcorn and mulled wine is more enticing than the most exquisite meals when one is huddled up in an igloo in Switzerland. It is impossible to articulate the frenzied rhythm of the Spanish *feria* in words! Or to describe the commotion inside one's head as one lets go of the last step of a ladder suspended deep in the sea in the Maldives. How can a travel writer describe the trepidation and elation one feels while being suspended so deep under the water that it's impossible to see anything except playful fish and hear anything except the sound of one's own breath. How? For that you need to get off that proverbial chair and travel. You need to let places seep into your soul till they talk to you.

If you're new to travelling, I would suggest starting small. Take a day trip or visit a city within your own country. Graduate to taking a trip to a neighbouring country or a different continent altogether – yes you will need to get visas issued, currency converted and spend ages trying to find the perfect accommodation. But it will give you a chance to learn about a new culture, exchange fascinating stories with strangers, cherish new friendships that will last a lifetime and try culinary delicacies that will leave you wanting more.

At each stage of your travelling journey, make sure you don't get too caught up in ticking things off a checklist or trying to pack your itinerary in a way that will leave you exhausted. The magic rule of savouring new places is to remember that there will be no Wi-Fi in that village of Morocco, rice and meat will probably be the only thing on the menu while camping in the Bolivian desert, snowstorms might cut short your Northern Lights expedition to Iceland and rains might disrupt your visit to Bali. But therein lies the secret to enjoying a new place too – surrender, give in to its whims, idiosyncrasies and the little things that make it special.

Surrender to days saturated with experiences. That's when Gibran's words will hit you. We've dedicated this section of the book to twenty such experiences, curated by both of us after exploring the length and breadth of the world. We hope they inspire you to take a leap of faith and experience a corner of the world in a different way this year!

1. Take a road trip in New Zealand

A summer road trip in New Zealand will take you through mountains surrounding symmetrical rows of fragrant lavender, sun-soaked beaches, the best hikes, hissing volcanoes and geysers spitting steam, and perfectly preened alpine villages. It truly doesn't get more scenic than this!

2. Go on an adventure in Bolivia

Bolivia is home to Salar De Uyuni, the largest salt desert in the world. Its remote location makes it ideal for seasoned travellers and photographers. If you enjoy thrilling experiences in the wild, this road trip is for you! We set off early one morning in a 4x4, stocked with water, food, snacks, gasoline and oxygen tanks, should we need them! We drove on barren land, pebbles and rocks for the next three days. There are no gas stations, shops, or roads here. Infrastructure is non-existent and the sights surreal.

This is one of the most remote, highest, and least-populated areas on Earth. There are no traffic signals here but every once in a while you have to halt the car to let the cutest llamas and alpacas cross the road! The best part? Close to the Chilean border, at 14,000 feet, lies Laguna Colorada – a red-coloured lagoon dotted with flamingoes. One of the most surreal natural wonders of the world, the water here is red because it houses algae that contain carotene, which photosynthesizes with the sun to lend it a red colour. The sunnier it is, the redder it is! This algae is ingested by flamingos, which gives them their pink colour. We kept feeling the two of us have walked into a National Geographic documentary.

3. Go offbeat in Europe

Slovenia is a tiny country and not an obvious choice for a road trip in Europe but it offers incredible panoramas at every step. You can expect historical towns rimmed by blue waters, unending vineyards punctuated with wineries and eateries, Alpine lakes that change colour every hour of the day and scenic villages surrounded by meadows as far as the eye can see – Slovenia is all that and more! The best part? It is one of the most affordable European countries – think Swiss panoramas at one-fourth the cost! With a side of glittering beaches too! Go lie on the beach, sail towards a castle, drive through mountain passes, or wake up in a glamping hut by the shores of Lake Bled.

4. Live like locals in your favourite part of the world

Most people rush to Europe when they take a gap year or a sabbatical from work. But instead of country-hopping, we would suggest choosing an affordable place where you can stay for longer. Places like Bali and Guatemala are ideal for this kind of slow travel if you're an Indian passport holder. Travel is not always about seeing new places or ticking countries off a checklist. Sometimes it is about living like locals, picking up a new language in a place you know well, stopping by at a neighbourhood eatery, or taking a day trip in the vicinity. It's about letting a place seep into your soul till it becomes a fibre of your very being. We have spent more than twelve months in the past few years in Bali and it has begun to feel like home to us.

5. Embrace Peruvian culture

Let me tell you a story about why you need to visit the villages of Peru for truly special encounters with Peruvians. The Andes have several charming villages and it is possible to spend entire days with local weavers in the Andean mountains – observing their craft, trying one's hand at weaving and occasionally sharing their lunch. While walking in this tiny village, I saw an old lady sitting by the stream of water, sifting chaff from quinoa. In my broken Spanish, I asked her if I could take her picture.

'Si,' came the answer, along with a nod.

When I finally clicked the photograph and went over to show it to her, she laughed as if it were the first time she had seen her own picture, her face blushing. And then she said, shyly, '*Uno más por favor* (One more please)!'

This time when I retreated to take her picture, I could see her eyes trained on the camera, the plate tilted to allow the grains to fall just so and a cheeky smile on her face. It turned out to be an amazing shot, and guess what, she nodded in agreement when I showed her this one. I asked her for her address and posted this photograph to her upon getting back to India. It's been years but I still can't get over her smile and the sparkle in her eyes. It's experiences like this that make travelling special.

6. Discover a little-known country

In the day and age of the mighty internet, it is hard to find surprises while travelling. Every little attraction has been documented or photographed by someone or the other. Perhaps that is why we enjoyed our trip to Azerbaijan so much – it was after a long time that we visited a country where there were surprises at every corner. We went expecting high-rises in Baku and historical treasures in the countryside. But we met amazing people, saw natural wonders, visited the northernmost villages of Europe and had some of the best meals while travelling.

As a former member of the USSR, Azerbaijan has a fraught history. The capital Baku has undergone a huge resurgence over the past ten years. Shopping malls, high-rises, luxury hotels and a picture-perfect promenade – you'll find it all here. But driving out of Baku is like stepping back into time. You will find historical treasures without another tourist in sight, natural wonders untouched by tourism and charming little mountain villages that seem to have sprung out of a postcard.

7. Experience Karnataka in all its glory

Did you know that between the months of July and September, the villages around Mysore are dotted with miles upon miles of sunflower fields? Plan a road trip that truly does justice to the diversity of Karnataka by visiting coffee and spice plantations around Coorg, the beaches of Gokarna and historical temples at Hampi. Tropical plantations punctuated with gold sunflower fields, modern highways flanked by marigold fields as far as the eye can see, neon green paddy fields surrounded by palm trees and hidden waterfalls – a summer road trip in Karnataka makes for a memorable getaway with friends and family.

8. Be seduced by Mexico

From sultry Mexican evenings spent dancing in the neighbourhood *cantina*, pub, to sampling salsa at a street-side eatery as a bead of sweat trickles down the nape of your neck, there is something deeply sensual about life in Mexico. Pink beaches, chilli flakes being sprinkled on juicy pineapples, local women flaunting bright *huipiles*, loose tunics, and flowers in their hair, sleepy towns with vintage Volkswagen Beetles lining the alleys, delicately spiced food eaten under sprawling trees on the roadside and crumbling Mayan ruins – we will never forget our trip to Mexico. Mexico is ideal if you enjoy stunning beaches with a side of history and scrumptious food.

9. Keep your cameras ready for Alberta, Canada

If you've ever wanted to visit a place just for spectacular landscapes and panoramas, then a road trip through Banff and Jasper National Parks in the Canadian province of Alberta is just for you. In fact, you can expect photograph-worthy scenes at every step. Driving from Banff to Jasper on the Icefields Parkway (Highway 93) is a dream for every road trip lover – this 230-km road is one of the most scenic roads in the world and with good reason! There are countless opportunities to picnic by gorgeous lakes, go glacier hopping, or hike on mountains covered by carpets of beautiful flowers. Don't miss Peyto Lake, which gets its milky turquoise hue from glacial silt.

10. *Marvel at aurora borealis in Lapland*

Reindeer sleigh rides, glaciers, igloos and the Northern Lights – a trip to Lapland is bound to be a once-in-a-lifetime adventure! If you have young kids or just like your holidays peppered with magic and fairy dust, then choose Finnish Lapland. Finnish Lapland is a truly phenomenal corner of the world. The air is clear (no pollution here!), water is sugary sweet, the sky sparkles with thousands of stars and the snow-laden landscape seduces people into thinking this is paradise. It could well be. Lapland is a winter wonderland where reindeer, huskies, scarlet sunrises and the Northern Lights all come together to create magic.

11. *Experience the soundlessness of Ladakh*

As we make our way to Ladakh, lush meadows, chinar forests and apple orchards give way to barren landscapes illuminated by the glimmering sun. Monks are everywhere and monasteries dot the landscape – that's when you know you've arrived in one of the most spectacular places on Earth! A journey in Ladakh is well and truly the stuff of dreams. Its soundlessness, its cobalt blue skies and glistening lakes are pure magic. This area boasts of iconic landmarks including some of the highest mountain passes in the world such as Zoji La and Tanglang La; splendid scenic drives in remote regions and some little-known gems such as the kaleidoscopic More Plains, Lamayuru and the hypnotic Gata Loops.

12. Get some exercise in Australia

Most people drive the Great Ocean Road, the legendary coastal route that passes through rainforests, quaint coastal towns, beaches and waterfalls. But we suggest hiking the entire stretch to get up, close and personal with the Australian Bush. Some of our favourite spots include panoramic viewpoints around Port Campbell, the Otway Lightstation (great for spotting koalas!) and the rural hinterland around Johanna. The stretch is peppered with great eateries spilling with fresh produce and some of Victoria's finest wines, so there are great rewards waiting for you upon completion of the hike.

13. Experience life in the shadow of Mount Fuji

A trip to Japan during cherry blossom season offers everything a tourist could possibly want from a country – sumptuous panoramas, bustling marketplaces, delicious food, safe and efficient public transport and helpful locals. Add to this entire bylanes and gardens full of powder-pink sakura petals and it becomes hard to argue with the prospect of planning a trip in Japan during spring.

Your getaway will start in the hustle and bustle of Tokyo but make sure you escape to Mount Fuji for a few days, explore the historic treasures of Kyoto and book yourself a chalet in offbeat Hakuba, often known as the Japanese Alps, for some peace and quiet.

14. Make merry in Spain

For a trip packed with endless sensory experiences, try visiting Spain during fiesta season, i.e., the month of August. Drive from Malaga all the way to Costa Brava via Granada, Valencia and Barcelona. Along the way, make merry at the *Feria De Malaga* in the south and fight with tomatoes at the Tomatina festival in Buñol. This is a trip with a dollop of crazy, and it's perfect if you're travelling with friends.

15. Switch up the seasons

Everyone rushes to Switzerland during the summer months but we suggest visiting during the winters to experience the country at its finest. Iconic mountain peaks, scenic chalets, quaint villages blanketed with snow, handcrafted cheeses, bespoke chocolates and some of the prettiest drives in the world – a winter trip in Switzerland ticks all the boxes!

16. Explore the backwaters of Kerala

Book yourself a stay on a houseboat in Kumarakom, a great alternative to the crowded Alleppey. This is an experience like no other. When you're booking, make sure you choose a traditional houseboat fashioned out of reed, cork and bamboo. Treat yourself to a canoe ride, a traditional Ayurvedic massage or go birdwatching. Expect to spend your time sailing past duck farms, busy villages and floating shops. Watch the sun set over the backwaters from the comfort of your houseboat and savour local delicacies such as meen pollichathu (grilled fish) or spicy karimeen curry and *sadya* (traditional vegetarian feast) as the day metamorphoses into night in front of your eyes. Spend evenings lounging on the boat while staring at the stars.

You can combine your trip to the backwaters with a visit to the beaches of Varkala or Kovalam, the tea estates of Munnar, or the spice plantations of Thekkady, depending on your preferences and the time you have at hand. Brightly coloured houses, reticent but smiling locals and undulating tea estates spread out as far as the eye can see – a trip in Kerala is a delightful assault to the senses – the colours, the smiles and the landscapes are bound to leave the traveller in you reeling with joy.

17. Get ready for an adventure in Sikkim

Glittering glacial lakes, endless pastures, waterfalls at every turn, quiet monastery towns and scenic drives on some of the worst roads we've encountered on our travels made our trip to Sikkim an adventure we will never forget. Mount Kanchenjunga peeking out from behind the clouds at Pelling, the surreal blue water of Gurundongmar Lake, one of the highest glacial lakes in the world, and the scrumptious momos at little hole-in-the-wall eateries in Gangtok, make the trip truly memorable.

18. Discover a romantic utopia in Fiji

Imagine a palm-fringed paradise. Devouring a meal as the sun sets over the ocean. Getting a rejuvenating massage to the sound of the waves. Swimming with baby sharks. Luxuriating in the splendour of villas far away from civilization. Fiji offers all that and more. What makes the archipelago special is the sensory experiences that are unleashed on guests the moment they step foot on the islands – white powdery sand tickles your toes persuading you to stay a little while longer, the creaminess of a coconut curry seduces the palette, its coral reefs tempt even amateur scuba divers, Fijian sunsets work hard to give you goosebumps and the sweltering heat seems to be there just to provide you with an excuse to take a dip in temperate waters that make your heart sing. So many sensations in one short evening – that's how Fiji makes its guests fall in love with the country! Ideal for a honeymoon or a special celebration with your partner.

19. Plan a once-in-a-lifetime experience in the Svalbard Islands

It is hard to get to Svalbard Islands, a Norwegian archipelago in the Arctic Ocean. But boy is it rewarding! You will fly to Longyearbyen airport, the northernmost commercial airport in the world and begin your journey. This is an experience that will leave you with visuals that will stay with you forever – floating icebergs, polar bears in the wild, rustic country lodges and almost twenty-four hours of daylight if you visit during summer months. This trip is ideal for cold-weather enthusiasts and bird-watchers.

20. Drive Iceland's iconic Ring Road

As we watched a colossal rainbow originating from the gorge next to the Skógafoss waterfall, we wondered whether Iceland was the proverbial pot of gold we've been told to look out for all our lives. It's hard to articulate what Iceland really feels like. Thanks to endless information on the internet, most travellers reach Iceland expecting surreal landscapes and picturesque panoramas. But nothing can prepare you for what lies in store on a road trip through Iceland. Within minutes of starting your drive, you will feel your spirits uplifted. The Earth is alive in Iceland – there are bubbling springs, effervescent rainbows, gurgling waterfalls, handsome horses and stunning mountains at every step.

Part 3

Living like Digital Nomads

7

THE DIGITAL NOMAD LIFE

On one of our very first trips to Bali, a Polish girl handed me a book after a long conversation about Love and Life in a tiny cafe. As I opened it I saw a sentence highlighted in neon pink, which summed up our hour-long conversation in just a line.

Don't be pushed around by the fears in your mind. Be LED by the dreams in your heart.

Here's how life usually goes – we educate ourselves, get a job and gradually get sucked into a routine. Despite nascent dreams we continue to live our lives, grumbling about our jobs but turning up at office every day in order to pay for a bigger car or a better house. We are repeatedly told that both ambition and success can only be measured in terms of career progression or the amount of money one earns. Over the years, this acquires the status of a 'fact' or a 'truth' through a series of reiterations – by parents, teachers, society, friends – you name it.

But balancing these priorities by choosing a unique career comes with its own set of challenges. You hear the phrase 'Dream it, work for it, live it' thrown around quite often on social media. In fact, it seems to be a favourite with us millennials, but what no one tells you is that the phrase is just half the truth!

Contrary to popular perception, it takes a lot of time, persistence and hard work to attain and, more importantly, sustain a location-independent model of living! Sleeping in a different bed every week, managing finances while trying to live your best life, sampling new cuisines every week and living out of a suitcase is hard but we love it to bits. And have so much fun at it that we have absolutely no complaints.

When we started blogging, over nine years ago, the digital space in India was unregulated. There were just a bunch of us, willing to step into the void and take a massive leap of faith. We were sharing our passions with the world in the hope of building communities of like-minded people. Over the years, the digital space has become the forerunner of promotional activities for everything ranging from Bollywood and beauty products to biscuits and detergent powders.

The unprecedented rise of digital media has left a lot of universities grappling for the right way to understand and teach MBA aspirants the nitty-gritties of the social media world. This is an ever-evolving industry and there is truly no better place to learn and equip yourself than on the job itself. Over the past nine years, we have absorbed our learnings from first-hand experience like sponges, if you may. We have had the best of experiences. But we have also had the worst. We've stumbled upon lifelong friendships but also learnt the bitterest of lessons. However, we are big believers that digital success isn't as elusive as it is made out to be. In fact, there is a ten-step recipe to digital success that I am about to share with you.

We will bare our hearts in this freewheeling exchange to share things we've never revealed before so you can all learn from our experiences. Think of this as a masterclass on building an audience on social media, leveraging your presence on social media platforms and charting a brand that is representative of you.

But more importantly, we will also talk about what sets this lifestyle apart from the humdrum of the corporate rat race, and how it is possible to be successful while living life on your own terms and at your own pace. Your best life is waiting for you, if you're willing to put your best foot forward.

8

10 STEPS TO DIGITAL SUCCESS

1. Vid: Take control of your life

Sometimes the smallest of tasks are the hardest. We live in a world that is flimsy. Diets that promise quick results. Beauty products that promise to cure acne in twenty-four hours. Relationships without baggage. Perhaps that is why this is the one millennial stereotype that gets reproduced everywhere, from Bollywood musicals to the most nuanced of web series – that millennials are whimsical, darting from one relationship to the other, one job to the other, looking for meaning, constantly in flux. It's also the stereotype that I dislike the most.

But I understand it is rooted in reality. Reality so real, it is almost tangible. The truth is you and I are all bombarded with so much information each day that it's hard not to waver from one thing to the other. One week fires in the Amazon incite us to make sustainable choices while the next, bushfires in Australia and riots in New Delhi fight for our attention. We want to be equally committed to raising funds for a sustainable future and nipping communal riots in the bud by sharing the right kind of information with our friends and family on social media. But multiply this onslaught of information by weeks, months and years, and it results in an existential lethargy of sorts. We might be 'woke' enough to care about everything all at once but somewhere down the line, this results in dilution and a distinct lack of results. They even have a term for it now – compassion fatigue. Have you ever been in this situation?

If you have, we're here to tell you to stop. We are the food we eat and in today's day and age, it is no exaggeration to say we are the content we consume, sometimes mindlessly. The irony of our times is that in order to take a leap of faith and take true control of your life, you have to take a gargantuan step back. Unless you do so, digital noise will ensure you hop from being semi-passionate about one hobby to being semi-passionate about another hobby. And before you know it, days will melt into months and months into years. At the end of it, a dull ache is all that will remain.

But there are two secret ingredients that can help you shake off this dull ache and achieve everything you've dreamed of, and much more – commitment and persistence. A combination of these two magical ingredients is all that you need to quell the digital noise.

A lot of self-help books might tell you to inculcate the get-up-and-go attitude in order to succeed. But what they often leave out is that this does not happen overnight. It takes immense amounts of patience and a conscious remodelling of one's mindset over a long period of time. But the right amount of commitment and persistence can make your dreams come true, whatever your circumstances may be.

This intense focus on achieving your dream life isn't just a bent of mind. You can hone it in several tangible ways

- Make lists
- Create a vision board

- Stop consuming content mindlessly
- Set short-term goals and long-term goals, and achieve them, one step at a time.

Perhaps it is best to give you an example from my life.

My stripped-back childhood, devoid of any mollycoddling, might have its disadvantages. But it had its fair set of advantages too. Being treated like an adult from a very young age meant I had immense clarity of mind, even as a teenager. I always craved to make friends with people from all over the world. I was only sixteen when I secured admission to a university in Singapore for my undergraduate degree in computer science. Despite getting into the prestigious Indian Institute of Technology (IIT), I chose to move to Singapore to pursue my engineering degree. Turning down the more lauded institution in order to thrive in a cosmopolitan environment – commitment.

But it was not as simple as it sounds. International education is expensive and I did not want my family bearing that expense for me. So I weighed my odds, secured a small scholarship, and took a huge loan from a local bank, knowing full well that I would have to pay every penny of it back myself. Over the next few years, I worked odd jobs – teaching maths to school kids – to finance my education. I took up a job right after finishing university to hasten paying back the loan and it was almost seven years after I first decided to study in Singapore that I repaid the loan in its entirety – persistence!

Yes, I had taken a leap of faith all those years ago in choosing to relocate to Singapore. Yes, it needed endless commitment and persistence as a teenager to fulfil that goal, but those seven years are also the years that changed my life. In retrospect, it was well worth it.

It was in Singapore that I would realize I thrive when I meet people from across the world. It was there that I would discover that learning about different cultures and sampling different cuisines excites me more than anything else in the world. And it was there that I took my first international vacation with Savi.

Whilst I was at my first job, she would try to visit for short periods of time, and we would go backpacking to whichever place we could afford – Malaysia, Indonesia, Thailand. I had never been outside India till I somehow found myself pursuing an undergraduate degree in Singapore. So, it was Singapore that introduced me to the joys of travelling with the love of my life.

Seven years of commitment and persistence had paid off. I met some of my best friends – from France, Italy and China – in Singapore! They were all there to study or work. But that wasn't all. I had not just made friends from all over the world – I had achieved a lot more in this little country. I was beginning to fall in love with travel –

something that would become a very important part of my life in the years to come.

2. Savi: Own your struggles

It's no secret – the world of social media is a crowded place. Content creators are a dime a dozen, users are increasing every second, and anybody who is not on social media incites reactions ranging from surprise to disdain. Over the last ten years alone, the number of users on social media has tripled – according to the most recent surveys close to 4 billion people use social media.* So what is everyone doing on social media?

Most people are following trends and pouncing on trending hashtags. Everyone is sharing the highlights of their lives and, very often, curating a reality that may not exist. Our preened realities and the illusion of perfection have led to a spate of research about the ill effects of social media. Several studies indicate that Instagram has increased demand for everything from cosmetic treatments like lip surgeries to unrealistic body types through self-abusive practices like anorexia. But I firmly believe the majority of mental health issues that platforms like Instagram have

---

* https://backlinko.com/social-media-users#how-many-people-use-social-media

been blamed for arise from one simple issue – the herd mentality.

As a professional content creator, that is exactly what you want to avoid. Aping a fashionable celebrity or a trending blogger will only get you so far. If you truly want to stand out in the herd, then own your struggles. Having spent many years studying the ins and outs of social media, I firmly believe staying authentic and celebrating your struggles is the only shortcut to being successful while maintaining your mental health and sanity in the manic world of social media.

Talk about the best parts of your life, cherish the triumphs and acknowledge the wins. But never shy away from articulating the struggles. In fact, let your struggles shine – they will set you apart from the herd.

Of course, this process isn't as simple as it sounds. As human beings, we are programmed not to share our vulnerabilities in public. As kids, we are repeatedly told lying is bad. And then, quite ironically, we are conditioned to lie on a daily basis by pretending we have everything together. It's this conditioning one has to un-learn in order to speak about struggle on a public platform.

You need to come to terms with the fact that your hardships do not determine your future. In fact, they only make you more resilient. The truth is, you can craft your life exactly the way you want. And while you might think this is easier if you're socially or financially privileged, I feel it is adversity that makes you more determined to craft your life in a way that you are living your wildest dreams each day, whatever they might be.

I say this from experience. Today, we get questions about how we finance our travels ourselves on a daily basis. In fact, people even assume we come from really rich families. But that couldn't be further from the truth. I sat on a plane for the first time, gingerly, might I add, when I was eighteen – I travelled solo to attend an academic conference in Singapore. For my mom, that first airplane ride happened at the age of forty, because I really wanted her to see the university I studied in!

Growing up, my father, a doctor, and my mother, a homemaker, spent all their earnings to provide the best possible standard of living to my brother and me. So, when I left high school and entered university, I was determined to finance my own education so they could finally spend their earnings on themselves. I was passionate about English literature and I knew I wanted to pursue a PhD from one of the world's best universities. But I also knew my parents could never finance this dream of mine. And getting bank loans for an expensive degree in humanities isn't an option as it is hard to repay them on a university lecturer's salary.

I won't lie. At that time of my life, it seemed like there was no way out. There are long periods where I felt nothing was going the way I wanted it to go. But I was not willing to give up on my dream. In fact, this roadblock made me even more determined to achieve it all by myself.

I was a stubborn teenager. I had envisaged what I wanted from life and worked towards this in three ways. First, I tried to score the highest possible grades while pursing my bachelor's and master's degrees at the University of Delhi. I would work endlessly, even through festivals and weddings in the family.

Some years, I succeeded in topping the university but other years I would miss it by a mark or two. After completing my master's degree, I started my MPhil degree almost immediately. But I also started teaching at the University of Delhi to gain work experience and earn money for university applications. These were perhaps the longest days of my life – I was waking up at 4 a.m. to prepare lectures for work as I was juggling a full-time job as a lecturer, trying to complete an advanced degree and applying to foreign universities at the same time.

I spent everything I earned from my job to apply to as many universities as I could. I spent months honing my applications while trying to look for scholarships that would help finance my degree. In my enthusiasm, I would spend entire nights emailing professors at my favourite universities to discuss my research proposal with them. This was a lonely journey, as I had no one who could provide any direction to me at the time. So I did everything I could. Eventually, I got my dream scholarship at

University of Leeds, one of my tops picks. The scholarship was generous and I supplemented it with odd academic jobs such as teaching English to international students at my university and invigilating during exam season. But there was one catch.

Writing a thesis takes anywhere between five to six years but my scholarship would support me only for four years. I was ready for the long days and endless work for years, but I ended up finishing my PhD in just under four years.

Why am I telling you this here, in a book about travel blogging? I did not know it at the time, but the lonely journey of PhD applications, securing funding and writing my thesis holed up in a room, without socializing for months at a stretch, was teaching me important lessons – discipline, the importance of structuring my days well and setting my own goals. And perhaps, most importantly, the refusal to give up on one's dream bears fruit. This work ethic proved invaluable to me in the travel blogosphere. I was fortunate that my academic background prepared me for what lay ahead. But if you are an aspiring content creator or entrepreneur, I would really recommend honing these exact qualities in order to prepare yourself for being an entrepreneur because even on this journey, you will have no one to answer to but yourself.

Fast-forward a few years and it seems like my life is in order – I spend my days jet-setting around the world with the love of my life. It would be easy to pretend I have everything under control. But I never once want to share anything that isn't an authentic representation of my experience. I believe this is what connects our readers to Bruised Passports. So I frequently share stories of the hardships I've faced and continue to face. Even after years of shunning societal conditioning, it's hard to speak about adversity or the loss of a loved one. In fact, I cried many times over while penning the chapter about losing my father to a sudden stroke in this very book. But sharing your authentic self is also rewarding.

Once you learn to speak about your experience on a digital platform straight from the heart, without aping anybody or following the herd, something crazy will happen. You will stand out like a shining star. You will discover a community of like-minded souls, scattered across the world, willing to engage with your content, eager to contribute to conversations, and excited about the stories you share. This equilibrium is one every content creator should strive for!

Of course, this will help you garner an audience and eventually earn a sizeable income. But this simple process does a lot more – it will help you fight your demons and become a lot more confident in your skin. It will also make the process of crafting and curating content satisfying to you because you will not just be generating an income –

you will be adding meaning to your readers' lives. This will give you a sense of purpose larger than yourself and satisfy you in ways fame or money never will.

Instead of feeding the malaise that is infecting social media, you will actually use social media for what it was originally meant – to empower people to become the best versions of themselves and reach out for their dreams.

3. Savi: Educate yourself about finance and learn as much as you can

Let's talk about money and travelling. One of the most frequently asked question to travel bloggers and influencers on social media is, 'How do you finance your travels?' And I don't blame people for the curiosity!

If you want to turn your passion for an alternative lifestyle or creating content (whatever your niche may be) into a financially sustainable model, it's best not to be waylaid by quotes on the internet that promise nirvana on the lines of 'buy a one-way ticket and fall in love'. I learnt this the hard way! Coming from a background of arts and literature, I have had to educate myself about finances. It started with a stubbornness to keep track of personal accounts and file my own taxes. I truly wish they taught this stuff in school!

Gradually, the art of money management turned into a full-blown obsession with me. But of all the books and articles I have read, one line by Morgan Housel, an ex-columnist at *The Wall Street Journal*, which he wrote in his book *Psychology of Money*, has stayed with me:

> If you view 'do what you love' as a guide to a happier life, it sounds like empty fortune-cookie advice. If you view it as the thing providing the endurance necessary to put the quantifiable odds of success in your favour, you realize it should be the most important part of any strategy.

And he is right! A dream life, where you pursue what you love each day, sounds wishy-washy in isolation. You need to marry it with a financially promising model in order to make it sustainable. Realizing this will be one of the most important steps in your journey of digital entrepreneurship.

Do not transition to travel blogging or any form of digital entrepreneurship purely on a whim. Plan well. The honest truth is phrases like 'book a one-way ticket, get a tan, fall in love, never come back' sound good only on paper. In reality, travel and entrepreneurial expenses add up very quickly – so be smart. Everything from plane tickets to registering a company and securing a domain to maintaining a website, buying meals in foreign countries and employing people takes money. This is something those fanciful quotes often miss.

Both of us started working in our teens, because financial independence was always very important for us. So hard work was never a problem. But through careful financial planning we educated ourselves, travelled, saved for a travel fund and financed our entrepreneurial venture! And you can do the same – instead of using money, circumstance, or nationality as an excuse, see how you can overcome these barriers. Start small and work your way towards your dream. Before you know it your dream will become your reality.

That is why we are steering clear of dreamy clichés, omnipresent on the internet, and sharing 5 truly practical tips that have help you finance and realize your dream life:

1. Financial literacy is the most important asset for digital entrepreneurs. It is an important lesson in survival but unfortunately it is one that isn't taught in schools. The good news is we live in a world where it is easy to educate oneself through podcasts, audio books, workshops, even YouTube videos. As you work towards your financial independence, take some time to truly understand the stuff that is often designated as boring –

whether it is registering companies, paying taxes, computing savings, expense spreadsheets – inside and out. This will help you in managing your finances and laying out a practical framework for making your hobby your profession. The financial decisions you make from the moment you start earning, will shape your life. So it is important to be fully in control of those decisions.

2. Living beneath your means is underrated! As you work towards financing full-time travel or your own start-up, try to ensure you are saving an appropriate amount each month. You can calculate your savings and track your income and expenditure using a simple spreadsheet. According to the immensely popular 50/30/20 rule for money management, you should spend 50 per cent of your earnings on essentials such as rent, groceries and utility bills; 30 per cent on needs and indulgences such as shopping and dining; and save the remaining 20 per cent. But we believe that tracking your expenses and cutting back on indulgences like eating out or pub-hopping can raise your savings to 25–30 per cent of your income each month. When it comes to numbers, such little adjustments add up rather quickly! This

is also the easiest budgeting hack in the book that will help you envision and achieve your dream life.

This is a hack we used a lot when we first started earning. Cutting back on indulgences doesn't mean a life devoid of pleasure. You can rethink your indulgences and spend in a smarter fashion, depending on the stage of life you are at! This is why some of the first few trips during our early twenties involved a lot of backpacking in Asia – this was a convenient way to save a chunk of our salaries whilst still fanning our raging wanderlust. So cutting back in daily life is not as dreary as it sounds. In fact, it is rather exciting to be able to save more and see your dream of working full-time in travel come to life just by ordering fewer takeaways or spending lesser time on shopping websites.

And once your venture takes off, you will gradually make your way towards sustaining a profitable enterprise while spending as much as you would like on indulgences. Just make sure you are always living within or beneath your means, never over! This way you can live your dream life without having to depend on rich parents or any other magic pills. Always remember – you can do anything you envision if you dare to dream and approach it realistically.

3. If you have a dream life in mind, it is also very important to have lots of very honest financial conversations with yourself and your partner! Transparency about finances makes it easy to set goals alone or together and decide how to meet them. Something to note here is that these goals are always dependent on current circumstances and keep changing with time. This is why it is important to have micro and macro financial goals at each step. Think of these micro goals as steps of a ladder that will help you reach the top, i.e., your largest goal in life. If you make smart financial decisions in your teens and twenties, you will be much better equipped to fulfil all your dreams as you get older.

Let me give you an example: The two of us have wanted to travel full-time for as long as we can remember. But as teenagers, we were not financially stable enough to be able to do that. So we charted out a pathway, a ladder if you may, to our eventual goal – college degrees and good jobs that would help us save money for our travels and for financing our own start-up! So even though travelling was our larger goal, our micro goals at the time involved financing our own university degrees and securing jobs that would help us save money for our dream of travelling the world. And that was the only step of the ladder we concentrated on at the time.

4. Soon enough this little hurdle was crossed. It was time for the next stage. This next stage is perhaps the most important step of your financial journey, in the year 2021 more than any other time in history – A Rainy Day Sum. Once you start earning and saving, it is very tempting to throw caution to the wind and invest in your hobbies – be it buying an expensive camera or booking a trip to a bucket-list destination! We are here to tell you not to do that! Don't!

Instead, use a chunk of your savings and put aside a rainy day sum – most financial advisors suggest this sum should be able to sustain you for a period of six months. But as the recent pandemic has shown, this is nowhere near enough in a world wreaked with uncertainty. And pandemic or not, entrepreneurship is risky business, so it is important to err on the side of caution. As a rule of thumb, multiply your monthly expenses, no matter how little or much they might be, by twenty-four. That is your rainy day sum in a post-pandemic world. Keep it aside and do not touch it. That way you will pursue your dreams with the confidence that you could sustain yourself financially, in unforeseen circumstances.

5. Let the games begin! It is time to get the start-up you've been dreaming about under way. I would suggest starting small and investing only what you can personally afford – whether it's your time or your money. And gradually scaling up when the time is right.

   This debt-free approach might be controversial but over the years, we have realized it is what contributes to an immense peace of mind. Both of us come from families where mortgages, loans and EMIs were a strict no-no. It was simple – if you couldn't afford something, you didn't buy it! This was the reason my family would undertake the longest of road trips in a rickety Maruti 800, which was practically falling apart at its seams!

   Once we grew up, we realized a debt-free approach isn't necessarily the smartest strategy, given the current finance scape. So we tried to question our conditioning and break this cycle. But even the smallest of loans we took, whether it was for education or purchasing something, left us feeling terribly encumbered. Somewhere our upbringing had left an indelible mark. It was hard to shake off the feeling of being bound when we had EMIs to pay. And for us resolutely independent souls, that was a strict no-no! Gradually, we realized being debt-free truly contributed to our main aim in life – living meaningfully and living consciously.

This has led to some hard decisions – for example, despite advice by several financial experts, we decided we would never secure external funding or open our blog Bruised Passports to investors to earn greater profits! Purely because this external influence would dilute our vision and make us bound to a place by virtue of offices and teams.

For the two of us, at home in the world, it would clip our wings. Why am I sharing this here? Because smart financial decisions aren't always the ones that provide the maximum amount of profit. Sometimes they are the ones that help you sleep peacefully at night and pursue your passion with an outlook that is entirely your own, no one else's.

Now we only invest in assets, ventures and experiences we can afford in the moment. And I am still petrified of loans – thanks, Dad!

4. Savi and Vid: Be brave and take that leap of faith

Growing up, I never thought there was a seat for me, so I've decided to build my own table.

The words on Uzo Aduba's social media bio never did leave us. We grow up thinking confidence in our passion is very important and armed with that, we follow the footsteps of our role models, and break that glass ceiling. But what happens when we veer towards a profession that has no glass ceiling? No template? In fact, it isn't even considered a viable profession at all.

It is scary, to say the least. When we first started professional travel blogging, there were only a very small handful of people doing it all over the world. Unsurprisingly, most of them were white. Brown faces were few and far between and we faced a lot of hiccups because of that. During those days, we were constantly side-lined at international conferences. Despite producing the highest quality work possible, we would not be invited to esteemed travel events or trade shows because travel blogging was the bastion of the developed world. Tourism boards would not consider sending mailers to bloggers from developing countries because our markets were not deemed as important as they are today! It almost seemed like we had to work harder to prove ourselves just because of the colour of our skin and our nationality.

However, these challenges were nothing compared to the ones we faced while making our own family and friends understand our inclination for a practically non-existent profession. We had thought long and hard about our dreams of digital entrepreneurship. We had made wise financial decisions that would serve us well in the years to come. We were confident we would excel in a field where we could share each one of our passions with the world – travel, photography and writing!

But we will be honest – despite all these rational thoughts, the constant questioning by people close to us led to second thoughts, many times over. Well-meaning relatives asking us, 'You are both so educated – who leaves such well-paying jobs to blog?' Friends would reiterate, 'Travelling this much on an Indian passport is impossible.' 'What will you do when your savings run out?' 'What if you can't make this financially sustainable?'

This long list of 'What ifs' had us questioning our own choices. We even briefly considered giving up on our dream life. It was unnerving to quit our jobs, a safety blanket if you may, in a world that constantly told us we were being reckless. But we are both big believers of setting our own goals and letting our work ethic speak for itself – if you put in work and stick to your targets, you will achieve whatever you set out to do. And in doing so, you will automatically smash stereotypes and prove your naysayers wrong. So we thought long and hard, and did what we do best – in 2014, we took that leap of faith and it has been the most fulfilling feeling in the world.

This is a triumph we have often experienced on our travels. We remember being 150 kilometres north of the Arctic Circle wherein lies one of the most mystical and charming parts of Finnish Lapland – Yllas is a skiing destination that gets its name from a fell, and is steeped in local folklore. On our most memorable day in the area, we were up early to try our hand at ice climbing, followed by long hikes on snow-laden mountains. One would think the physical exertion would automatically translate to a good night's sleep.

But we were there also to experience the Northern Lights and the promise of the thus far elusive spectacle kept us awake! After a few hours of tossing and turning in bed, we looked at each other and knew we were both thinking about the exact same thing – we should go hunt down the aurora borealis! We gingerly stepped out of our lodge, heated our car and drove out of the tiny village into the Finnish wilderness. In a pitch-dark bylane, we put on some mellow music and decided to wait for the Northern Lights, huddled in our warm car. Forty minutes later, still no sign! Every time one of us would mention going back to the lodge, the other would dissuade. The aurora forecast was good but it seemed like Mother Nature had no intention of putting on a show!

At 3 a.m., we spotted another pair of headlights. Soon enough, a lone gentleman slowed down next to us, asking us if we were in trouble! He was on his way to work for an early-morning shift. We assured him we were okay – just two kids with wonder in their eyes hunting for their favourite Northern Lights.

And just then, more than two hours after we first got there, the sky lit up, green, purple, pink all at once! That night we witnessed our first 'Aurora Storm' – the most vibrant lights we've seen on our travels. Do you see? Leaps of faith, no matter how little or monumental, are always worth it. We had started the night feeling restless in our bed but we wound it up sipping on warm lingonberry juice with a complete stranger near the village of Yllasjarvi.

As entrepreneurs and content creators, we often dwell on several tangible parameters such as products, strategies and returns. But the truth is, in the nascent stages of digital entrepreneurship, it is this non-tangible leap of faith that is the toughest hurdle to cross. We hope this story will help you understand that nothing happens overnight. A lot of blood, sweat and tears go into making any dream a reality! But we also hope it will inspire you never to give up on your dreams – you can do anything you envision if you dare to dream and approach it realistically. Don't give up on your dream! Find a way to live it.

Growing up, I never thought there was a seat for me, so I've decided to build my own table.

Indeed!

5. Kid: Work it!

If you do choose to take that leap of faith and start your journey as a content creator, don't underestimate the amount of work full-time blogging takes! Blogging is a relatively new profession, so it is easy to look at curated social media feeds and envy the 'lucky' bloggers in question. Unfortunately, there are no free lunches in the world. Digital creators work very hard to create and curate content on a daily basis. Having experienced both sides of the coin now, we can confidently say content creation is a lot more demanding and time-consuming than the average desk job. Perhaps it is because you are your own photographer, stylist, writer, editor, PR manager – this list is endless. Even if they have some help along the way, most creators are closely involved in the entire process of producing valuable content, right from ideation to execution and sharing. This often is exhausting. But it is also more rewarding, so you will not regret choosing your passion even for a moment.

When we first started blogging, we worked ten-hour shifts at our website and social media every day alongside our day jobs (hello twenty-hour work days!). Hundreds of hours were spent garnering a readership on social media and our website. It was a steep learning curve and we picked up many lessons along the way. Finally, after over three years of doing this, we took the leap to travel full-time.

If you are also juggling content creation with a day job, we recommend spending your precious time to learn:

- The basics of digital marketing including Search Engine Optimization (SEO)
- To create authentic content
- To optimize hashtags
- The basics of designing websites, even if you choose to outsource it
- To work on brand partnerships
- The basics of affiliate marketing

In addition to these things, it is also important to take time to study your niche – whether it is fashion, interiors, travel, beauty, wellness, finance, technology or food. Spend your time on research and go as deep as you possibly can. See what is out there and how you can contribute to the conversation. Do not be discouraged if your niche is super specific – fragrances, third-wave coffee, candle-making, surreal art or vegan retreats. There is no better place to

connect with the people of your tribe than social media –
modern day pen pals if you will.

Irrespective of what your niche might be, do not feel
compelled to splurge on fancy equipment just to kickstart your career on social media. Instead, practice with
the existing equipment you have in your armoury – it is
easy to start a website or social media page with a free
membership and a mobile phone. Start small – if you
aspire to be a travel blogger, try to curate itineraries and day
trips from your hometown. Shoot photos of offbeat gems
and share your intimate knowledge of your hometown
and little-known facts about it with the world. If you're
a teenager with a keen eye for photography, looking to
make a mark on social media, use whatever equipment
you already own, even if it is just a mobile phone. Try
to acquaint yourself well with every single feature offered
by your phone and exploit different features to create a
portfolio that is impressive to an onlooker. In each case,
try to produce high-quality content that does justice to
your way of perceiving the world, whether it is through
articles, photographs or videos.

We followed each of these steps, listed above, in our
journey on social media. Despite that, our numbers did
not grow overnight. In fact, they grew gradually over a
period of five to six years. Something to remember when
you see our idyllic photos on the internet is that it took us

eight years of saving and three years of blogging alongside full-time jobs to transition to a location-independent model of working. And most of our peers, who are content creators, have similar stories. Even now, when Bruised Passports is nine years old, we work longer hours on it than we used to in our jobs. So don't expect quick returns. The process of success in the digital world is gradual but the journey is smattered with many highs such as making friends along the way, collaborating with like-minded people, and garnering knowledge about an area you are passionate about.

Besides, the beauty of travel blogging as a profession is that relishing new corners of the world keeps the excitement alive. Over the years, we've had dozens of memorable experiences on our travels. But there is one night that always stands out because of the unexpected way in which it unravelled! We were on a road trip in Spain – we booked this trip specially so we could write about the carnival season in the country and share a detailed itinerary with our readers. We spent the month driving along the coast, partaking in the revelry, dancing our hearts out at street parties and drinking some of the best (and worst!) sangria in the world. We made friends and pelted each other with tomatoes in the largest food fight in the world – La Tomatina. We learnt the flamenco, well … somewhat! On a cloudy evening, we drove along the coast and up to our rental apartment in Costa Brava

– a quaint cottage covered with ivy and a small gazebo surrounded by grape vines. I had seen photos on AirBnB, so I recognized it the second we pulled into the street. We called up the host, so we could collect the keys and get settled in. No response! This happened thrice.

We had started looking for other options online to no avail – everything was booked to capacity because of the carnival. Then the phone rang. Our host, a twenty year old, had 'forgotten' we were arriving and was away for the weekend with his friends. In true Spanish fashion, he said, 'My father lives two blocks away, why don't you go and relax at his place, I'll be there first thing tomorrow.' Then the last blow, 'Oh and he doesn't speak much English.'

I'm a stickler for planning so I couldn't quite believe what we were hearing. But I also knew we didn't have much of an option – it was already 9 p.m.! So off we went to the *padre,* not knowing what to expect! Sure enough, a rickety bed in a crumbling colonial home awaited us. We were about to hit the sack when we heard a knock – the old man was standing with a bottle of Andalusian sherry and scotch! All of us tiptoed on to the balcony – a charmingly cluttered space full of plants, old furniture and melted candles. We made ourselves at home around a tiny patio table on rustic chairs with ivy entwined around the legs.

First round – a stiff drink and a colourful tale about his wayward son's irresponsible behaviour. Second round – a stiffer drink and tales about the Spanish Civil War – in Spanish and broken English. Third round – the stiffest drink yet and we were telling him tales in English and whatever smattering of Spanish we had picked up along the way. This was at 12 a.m. We never did sleep that night. We spoke about everything from colonization and languages to senility and youth. We found ourselves enamoured by tales of his youth and goaded him to tell more!

The next day, his son came and checked us into the house we had originally reserved. We partied a lot on that trip and met so many new people along the way but there was not another night like that first one! Can you guess whether we left a negative review or positive review for the host?

6. Savi: Time management and discipline

I truly feel that most handbooks about creative professions never talk about some uber-traditional values that are most essential in such professions – perhaps because it is more fashionable to sell the idea of whimsical artists than hardworking professionals?

Take, for instance, the importance of discipline or consistency in a career on social media. Did you know shooting images or providing valuable information via videos, captions and articles is immensely time-consuming? But even so, that is merely the tip of the iceberg when it comes to content creation.

If you are a budding content creator or aspire to be one, make sure you are present on most major social media platforms and receptive to new players in the market. For example, Clubhouse is an increasingly popular social media app and when you are amongst the first to join a trending app, you have the distinct advantage of being the frontrunner in your niche on that particular app.

Also make sure you take the time to delve into insights that are available to creators on apps like Instagram and Facebook. This little exercise will help you figure out what time of the day your audience is most active and the kind of content they enjoy.

Additionally, make sure you vary your content depending on the platform and format. Let's take the example of Instagram:

- The Stories feature is ideal for more casual videos which disappear in twenty-four hours
- IGTV is for detailed videos which can be aesthetic yet packed with information
- Feed posts feature an array of photographs and videos which showcase the world through the eyes of the creator

- Static posts are apt for sharing highlights of your work
- Instagram Reels feature is reserved for shorter, snappier videos and entertaining bite-sized content

I don't blame you if you feel your content is more suited for one feature over the other. However, I would suggest maintaining diversity, not just for the sake of algorithms but also to challenge your own boundaries – this way you will get a chance to showcase your work in ways even you hadn't ever envisioned. In the world of ever-evolving media, this adaptability is very important and can make or break content creators. Make sure you view new features and new platforms with curiosity and an open mind instead of contempt or disdain.

Perhaps most importantly, post consistently. Try to post at least once a day, especially when you are trying to build your audience. While this sounds easy, it requires intense amounts of time management and discipline to do this on a regular basis. For example, if your audience is most active at 4 p.m. IST, try to post at the time and engage with your readers after you post. This could mean cancelling an ongoing meeting or setting an alarm for as early as 4 a.m. if you are travelling in the US or Peru – learn to see this not as a disruption of your daily schedule but an important part of your job as a content creator.

Engaging with your audience after posting a YouTube video or Instagram post is akin to following up on a project after its release in a corporate job. You should be there for it and your presence will, in turn, contribute to a growth in numbers and engagement. So the three things you must do if you are serious about a profession as a digital content creator would be to:

- Adapt quickly to newer formats and apps
- Diversify content
- Post as consistently as you can

As a digital content creator, this digital footprint also functions as your portfolio or CV in many ways. So it is important to be producing content that does justice to your vision while being consistent. Except the occasional digital detox, most content creators push out content 365 days of the year, sometimes multiple times a day – for unlike other professions, digital content curation is a job without holidays.

But perhaps we can all do that without burning out because it is also a job one doesn't need a holiday from. One of the perks of creating a location-independent lifestyle is that we can work from anywhere in the world, as long as there is Wi-Fi! That's why we've spent more than fifteen months in the past couple of years in Bali. Every time we are quizzed about why Bali feels like home to us, we think of our very first day on the island.

We booked a beautiful villa, overlooking the paddy fields, in the highlands near Ubud. Upon checking in, the host told us about a celebration at the neighbourhood theatre. On our first evening, we had planned to visit a waterfall, followed by dinner at a restaurant that came highly recommended by friends (and TripAdvisor). The plan was to nip into the community celebration for a while and leave.

But upon getting there, we were startled by the crowds. The atmosphere was akin to that of the Ram Leela grounds back home. It seemed like locals from all the nearby villages had congregated for the enactment. Vendors were selling snacks and cotton candy. Kids were busy buying balloons and little toys. Thoroughly intrigued, we entered the venue just as an enactment of the Ramayana was starting. Within minutes, we were surrounded by people on all sides and it became virtually impossible to leave the crammed venue!

We would go on to spend months exploring Bali's gorgeous waterfalls, hiking to volcanoes, working from our balcony, cooking Indonesian food in our kitchen and walking through endless paddy fields without a care in the world. But the memory of that first evening lingers on.

First days on most trips are spent perusing the highlights of the place or visiting its most famous attractions. But in

Bali our first evening was spent crammed like sardines in a local theatre, watching a rendition of the Ramayana in a language we did not understand. It was also the day we first met our host's son, who is now like a godson to both of us.

That is why I say it is a job I don't need a holiday from. Thanks to our profession, we can spend even the most ordinary work days in surroundings that leave us absolutely wide-eyed in wonder. Perhaps these micro stimulations, which us travel bloggers receive on a daily basis, ensure that intense discipline comes easy to us?

7. Vid: Building a digital brand that speaks volumes

It is no secret – whether you're a blogger, small home-owned business or an established name in the industry, digital is the future. Industry insiders always knew this focus on digital media wasn't a momentary 'boom' that would come crashing down. But skyrocketing sales on online portals during the COVID-19 pandemic has laid it out for everyone to see – digital media and e-commerce platforms are not a fad. They are symbolic of a fundamental shift in consumer behaviour. I spoke about expecting a gradual increase in numbers but in today's changing digital landscape, even the smallest of creators and entrepreneurs can expand phenomenally on the internet within a matter of weeks.

With the number of social media users rising each day, digital platforms will increasingly continue to affect each aspect of our lives – dining decisions, travel decisions, shopping decisions, health decisions – the list is endless. Of these, travel is one of the most popular categories for user-generated content as a large majority of people tend to share images and experiences on social media when they go on vacation. Did you know that over 70 per cent of travel decisions are made upon perusing photographs of gorgeous destinations and drool-worthy travel experiences on Instagram? I know for a fact my mom is one of those consumers because she often sends me screenshots of beautiful places nudging me to add them to my bucket list.

In such a saturated and ever-growing landscape, it is important to flesh out a distinct identity for yourself as a digital entrepreneur and content creator. While on the face of it, it might seem like numbers are the only way to gauge popularity, this is not true at all. Digital media is a much more nuanced industry today than it was a few years ago. Everyone, from companies and PR firms to your content creator peers, will look at a series of other metrics to gauge the impact you are having on the digital landscape. Factors such as engagement rates, ROI (Return on Investment), niche and the uniqueness you bring to the table count more than you would imagine. In fact, I envisage the focus on pure numbers to drastically decrease in the years to come.

This is why your emphasis should be on caring about your audience and you can do this in one simple way – by adding value, not spam, to the digital universe. If you are a Bruised Passports reader, you would know we do not ever celebrate numbers or hanker for felicitations – in fact, as many of you might know, we do not even attend award ceremonies or encourage our readers to vote for awards that are determined purely by numbers. That's because it's not the awards or accolades that will be crucial to your journey as a content creator – it will be your connect with your audience. In the world of content creation, your bond with the audience is the one that should be considered sacred and treated with the maximum amount of respect possible.

When we first started blogging nine years ago, there were only a handful of us talking about travel worldwide. There weren't any travel couples around. Now many years have passed and travel is a trending topic, which is incredible to see. Content creators are popularizing destinations that were previously not on travellers' radars. There are millions of user-generated photos in beautiful locations around the world.

Of course, this is not all pleasant – this has also led to content for the sake of content – cut-throat competition and an ugly underbelly has arisen that is almost impossible to ignore. There is also a lot of noise, much ado about nothing, if you will – we have personally witnessed authors on travel websites writing about places they've never visited and providing factually incorrect information to readers. This is not a stray instance, rather a pattern. This omnipresence of half-baked information online is practically dangerous. The irony is, there are millions of articles and posts out there but information that is truly useful to readers is even rarer than it was nine years ago!

That is the reason why you should never feel intimidated or think of the digital world as saturated – whether you're a photographer, creative graphic artist, barista or consultant – if you are keen on sharing your passion and your art, there is a place for you. But there is one thing you must remember. Irrespective of whether you focus on entertaining your readers, teaching them or providing tips – try to ensure you emphasise on providing true value to your audience and everything else will follow, including brand partnerships.

Due to our background and experience, we are frequently hired by brands as social media consultants and I can share this with you – in this increasingly streamlined industry, brands think twice about working with creators who endorse anything and everything. Going forward, brands will only get savvier. They will want content creators who care deeply about their audience and truly value the brand before endorsing it blindly or jumping onto a competing brand within the span of a month.

For this reason, one of the most important ways in which you can build your digital brand as a content creator is by maintaining your individuality on social media. Viewers and readers have been seeing stock photos from tourism boards, hotels and restaurants for years. They want subjectivity. They subscribe to content creators because they love to hear about authentic experiences, pros and cons, the good tales, and the bad ones. Most of all, they want to hear about the experience and the little tips that will help them along the way, were they to visit the same place.

Let me share a story with you – if I take off my blogger hat for a moment and look at travel blogging as a consumer, I can spy two distinct camps of travel bloggers. The first camp puts out well-researched articles on travel destinations but loves to dismiss social media as being superficial or fleeting. The second camp relies heavily on social media and puts out gorgeous inspirational photos but steers clear of offering any practical tips to their readers. In our opinion, the first camp offers valuable advice to their readers through their articles but their dismissive attitude towards social media and lack of adaptability to new mediums of dispersing information often nips their career trajectories in the bud. The second camp, whilst popular on social media due to their beautiful imagery, offers little to no practical advice to their readers.

As avid consumers of travel-related content, this is the gap we wanted to fill as content creators. With my love for photography, Savi's love for writing, and our collective vision of looking at the world through rose-tinted but also practical glasses, we wanted to put out beautiful photos of the world as we saw it but also provide detailed guides and essential tips to our readers who might want to visit the same places as us.

Our adventures and misadventures have provided fodder for these tips along the years. I remember the time we arrived in Europe, our eyes swimming with visions of glittering lakes, tall mountains and idyllic villages. This was our first cross-country road trip and we were there to experience the crisp autumn days in France and Switzerland. We rented our car at the Charles De Gaulle International airport in Paris, opting for the basic package, frowning over the bizarrely high surcharge for add-ons like snow tyres or 24x7 help. The first few days flew by as we drove through the French countryside – it was a vision at that time of the year – avenues full of fiery orange trees and parks laden with yellows and rusts. On day five, we crossed over into Switzerland. We drove through stunning mountain passes, picnicked in meadows and visited more chocolate factories than we care to remember. The Swiss countryside, we were convinced, couldn't get more picturesque.

On day nine, we decided to drive to alpine villages to witness the glorious scenery we had heard so much about. In retrospect, the smattering of snow started almost as soon as we got off the highway but we were too enamoured by the uphill drive to notice much. Approximately ten minutes later, we found our car stuck in snow in the middle of the busiest road of the village. It refused to move, no matter what we did! As the honking and grumbling from the cars behind us increased, we found ourselves going tomato red in the face! Oh well, you live and learn! Eventually a few helpful locals stepped in and we had to push our car out of the snow, the good old-fashioned way. But it took ages and we caused a huge traffic jam in a tiny little Swiss village in the process.

There is no cliché truer than: 'Travel is the greatest teacher.' That day we learnt this the hard way. Now we advise all our readers to pay an additional surcharge for snow tyres in the area, even if the amount might seem bizarre at the time of booking.

First-hand experiences and tips like these have now become our trademark. Gorgeous imagery corroborates guides as long as 5000 words sometimes. We wanted something that straddled the gap between the two mindsets I mentioned and offer something no one else put forward at the time. And we can say with certainty today that we've done just that. But when I look back on it, I am confident that the pieces of the puzzle fell into place because we decided to stick to our strengths and bring our individuality into the mix instead of following the herd and sticking to one of the two trends that were emerging at the time – quality articles or aspirational imagery.

This is why it is important to let your individuality shine. Nobody else is you and that is your power. Each day, your audience comes to your page to hear what you have to say, not what ten other people are saying at the same time. At this stage, I would like to propose a short exercise – whether you are a digital entrepreneur or not, join me in saying out loud a few things that make you special as a person. In fact, share the qualities that make you special using the hashtag #BPBook and we would love to reshare them with our readers.

As the digital landscape of India goes through a fundamental shift, it is important to keep reminding yourself that your story is important to your brand of digital entrepreneurship and content creation. If you want your story to be heard, you will have to celebrate both the strengths and hardships – mental or physical – that make you special. As you build your digital brand, make sure you remind yourself to relish your messiness and be fascinatingly individualistic. Don't change yourself to fit in. There is a special place for you out there on the internet – go create it!

8. Savi: Turning windfall loss into opportunity

It would be unfair to have an entire list dedicated to the ingredients of digital success without talking about the two years gone by. The years that have been the embodiment of most entrepreneurs' nightmares!

So far we have touched on many aspects that are important for any successful digital entrepreneur – SEO, digital marketing, the process of content creation, tips for curating content, working with brands, audience engagement and ROI. We've also spoken about the sheer joy of creating, especially as a travel blogger.

When you create, you get to catalogue your visits to little corners of the world and precious memories in new countries for posterity. What's more, you relive the experience every time you relish the content you created. Reading about strange encounters in Croatian forests sends a tremor down your spine. Looking at videos of Azerbaijan's villages makes you dream about road trips in the mountains. Going through photographs of Lake Atitlan makes you smile from ear to ear. But what happens when life throws a curveball that knocks you flat? The COVID-19 pandemic did just that, for us and many other entrepreneurs. Could any of us have envisaged a world where travelling would just stop – flights would be suspended, airports would be closed, and in an unforeseen display of the sheer unpredictability of life, travel would be deemed illegal?

With the entire world in lockdown, what were travel bloggers to do? We had important projects lined up for quite a few months, all of which were cancelled. We had big plans for 2020, including the launch of a product line, which were all stalled.

For the first couple of weeks, we stayed patient. Our work stopped completely but we continued to keep an open mind and practise gratitude for what we did have – our health and getting to spend quality time with each other. At this point it might also be imperative to issue a quick reminder of something I mentioned earlier in this book. Remember the rainy day fund? It is for situations like these that one should never disregard the importance of good financial planning.

For a while we stayed in our own little bubble – annoyed at the course of events but also thankful for hot meals and each other. In fact, it is at such times that one realizes the importance of spending your life with someone who sparks your soul. Nothing compares to the comfort of a love you can depend on through thick and thin – companionship is truly the most sacred of needs.

But as time wore on, we grew restless. The path to unlearning conventional wisdom, which is passed through generations, is never an easy one. But even after you have traversed it, carved out a niche for yourself and succeeded at what you set out to do, it is natural to be reminded of the naysayers when things go south. That was what happened with us, fleetingly, during the time of the pandemic. 'Digital entrepreneurship is not a viable career option and if anything went wrong – you will have only yourselves to fall back on,' they had said. Were they right all along?

These thoughts haunted me for a few days till I realized it wasn't true at all – even friends with the most stable jobs had unfortunately been laid off, established businesses were floundering, brick-and-mortar stores were closing down. These were unprecedented times, the world economy was bleeding, and everyone was suffering, especially entrepreneurs.

It was sometime around the three-week mark that we decided we would make this time count. The fortunate or unfortunate thing about juggling so many roles as a content creator is that the hunger to dream, create and do things is insatiable.

Adaptability is the cornerstone of any entrepreneurial venture, and as travel came to a standstill we decided to focus our energy on projects that were nascent little ideas, unable to take shape due to our schedules and constant travelling. With nowhere to go, we decided to use our time constructively to convert this windfall loss to newer opportunities, ones that would have been hard to mould, plan and design if the pandemic had never happened. Neither of us wanted to look back at 2020 with any regret.

First we decided to jump back on the content creation train by curating a series of images and videos inspired by our travels within the confines of the tiny one-bedroom apartment we were renting in London – a recipe we learnt in Morocco, an ancient proverb we picked up in Peru, forgotten photographs from a tiny shrine in Japan – this was the perfect time to share them all with our family of travel lovers, who were confined to their homes and missing the freedom of hopping onto a flight to visit a place that had tickled their fancy for months. We were aware none of us could venture to the great outdoors but there was nothing stopping all of us from taking little flights of fancy within the confines of our home by cooking an exotic dish or learning a new dance technique.

It was at this time we also got to work on our book, which you are reading today. Not moving around or packing and unpacking constantly freed up a lot of headspace, which allowed us to truly delve into the deepest corners of our hearts and minds and share these intimate details about our journey with you. Details we have never shared with anyone, except our closest friends and family.

As I continued to pen this book, details, which I had forgotten about, came flooding back from the tiny crevices of my mind. I cried while revisiting losses that made it hard for me to breathe, I smiled while thinking about the mistakes we had made when we first started travelling, and I promised myself to go back to Lake Atitlan for a few months – I had forgotten just how special it is. I hope you are enjoying reading our story because writing this book made me fall in love with the process of travelling and the concept of location-independent entrepreneurship all over again. I got reminded of the rush I felt when we first transitioned to a career in travel – it felt a bit like falling irrevocably in love with someone who is just right for you.

Perhaps the most challenging project we undertook at this time was the colossal **Bruised Passports App**. This is an idea we have had for a long time – a portal that would collate all our posts, articles and videos from across Instagram, YouTube and our website in a way our readers could consult it on the go, while on their travels. But we wanted to take it a step further and provide the exact coordinates of our photographs along with detailed information about the time of day ideal for shooting it and the camera settings needed for it. Years of interacting with our readers made us realize that many of them, especially those with busy jobs and large families, might not have the time to research these things before visiting a destination, so we wanted to make the process as simple and accessible as possible. But that wasn't all – we also wanted to include a playful scratch map, which could help our readers keep track of the number of countries they had visited. And finally, a series of presets that could help our readers edit photographs in minutes. Ideating this app was a lot of fun – we simply had to see how we could provide maximum value to our readers and make the process of exploring a new place as easy as possible.

But when it came to execution, the Bruised Passports App was no cakewalk. We spoke to a number of app designing firms and we were told that to create this app would be like creating three separate apps and collating them in one app – as a result, timelines were long and the investment much higher than we anticipated. This was why we shelved the idea for a while. But with the pandemic looming large, it was the perfect time to revisit our dream of having a portal that would make travelling easier for our virtual family. We were unwilling to compromise on the features – in fact, in the months we had shelved it, we had come up with a few more user-friendly features that we wanted to include in the final version. But with the pandemic, we had time. The world was confined to Zoom meetings, but that didn't stop us from looking for a team that would help us design our app and make our vision come to life. There was a risk – investing money into a new venture at a time when work was at a standstill. But a spate of number crunching later, we decided we would do it! I think that is because both of us realized if we did not do it at the time, our dream of having an app would never see the light of day. What followed was months of long workdays and endless conference calls. The process was a lot more tedious and time-consuming than either of us had anticipated but I couldn't have thought of a better time to do this – this is how, gradually, the Bruised Passports App began to take shape.

While we share a lot of our finished work online, this journey from conception to creation of projects is a part of our work that you rarely see online on social media. But I hope this behind-the-scenes look at the process of turning discouraging periods of windfall loss into opportunities will give you inspiration to multitask as a digital content creator.

But creating such opportunities and avenues shouldn't be limited to just times of loss. In fact, as a digital content creator, you should constantly work towards diversifying your streams of income by creating multiple sources of revenue. Think of diversifying your entrepreneurial portfolio in the same vein as diversifying an investment portfolio – investing in property, stocks, NFT, mutual funds and fixed deposits instead of putting all your eggs in one basket.

And this doesn't just apply to times of adversity. As an online content creator, you should refrain from putting all your eggs in one basket and think of diversifying in order to have more than one source of income to rely on. Some of the most popular streams of income you should look at as a digital content creator are:

- Affiliate links
- Product sponsorships
- Contributing to magazines and newspapers
- Contributing to websites
- AdSense revenue via YouTube and your personal websites
- Conducting workshops or providing mentorship as a result of your digital presence
- Providing consultations to brands within your niche

In addition to that, we would also encourage you to use your digital presence as a springboard to establishing something that you are passionate about. Perhaps you are a dancer and sharing your talent online can help you open a dance academy. A home baker who can use social media to network and start a chain of patisseries. Or a passionate graphic designer, who can kickstart a bespoke stationery business, upon gaining traction on social media. The opportunities are endless – all you need to do is seize them and put in the effort required to make them a reality.

Even though COVID-19 was traumatic in unprecedented ways, such unique ebbs and flows are a part of any entrepreneurial journey and content creation is no different. Pandemic or no pandemic, there will be many times when you feel like giving up. At times like these, unrelenting self-reflection and surrounding yourself with people that empower you and give you the right advice – mentors, friends, parents – will see you through. It goes without saying – you will face several hurdles while trying to make a mark in creative professions. Make sure you take the leap with a heart of steel, strengthened further by a practical approach and an undying passion to make it work. That is the holy trinity that will see you through good times and the crazy ones!

9. Vid: Defining success and learning to think in a world that is telling you to 'hustle' constantly

This here is the life, the life we once dreamt of designing for ourselves.

At this point, I could insert a travel cliché here about how millions of experiences make you richer than the wealthiest people on earth. But that simply is not true for everyone. In our case, Bruised Passports was a no-brainer given my love for photography, Savi's passion for writing and our shared fondness for travelling.

But the truth is not everyone enjoys constant travel, living out of suitcases, sleeping in a different bed each week, sampling new cuisines every day, working in new locations constantly, or making new friends regularly.

Having been on both sides of the coin, I can tell you one thing. There are no rights and wrongs when it comes to carving the life of one's dreams. There is no standard template either because every individual's dream looks different. Whether you choose to work towards a materially rich lifestyle, or leave everything to meditate in a forest, or travel the world – each choice has its pros and cons, and don't let anyone tell you otherwise.

Our advice? Try to experience everything in small doses and choose that one lifestyle that makes you happiest.

Once you find what makes you happy, have the courage to take the leap and the determination to see it through. So don't chase some version of happiness just because it's deemed cool by social media these days. Chase 'your' happiness – that unique equation that makes your heart sing each morning.

Of course, this is easier said than done in a world where we are often told that standard markers such as bigger cars, better houses and stable jobs are tantamount to success. In India, we grow up hearing very rigid definitions of ambition and success, which leave no room for flexibility. You might associate this with conservative thinking because the creative world is often romanticized to be different from this 'rat race' described above. As an insider, I can tell you the entrepreneurial world is no different.

In the entrepreneurial world, the traditional concept of success is often encapsulated by a word that can often veer towards being toxic – hustle! The traditional rat race is replaced by the constant pressure to juggle businesses, increase numbers on social media and be the embodiment of #entrepreneur, jumping from meeting to meeting. It is endless! The pressures are the same as before – in fact, many times, they are multiplied manifold as content creators' lives take place in the public eye.

As humans, we constantly tend to want something bigger, better, more. That psychology binds all of us. This is why it is important to take a step back and question this conditioning to see what really makes us happy. Reflect on the things that truly matter. In the process of unlearning everything you've been taught, you might discover what your definition of success actually looks like.

I am in no way saying money isn't important. Money pays bills. Money ensures a seamless life. As we mentioned earlier in this book, smart financial decisions are very important. But money doesn't have to be the be-all and end-all of one's life. Besides, as we have demonstrated in this book, it is possible to marry one's dreams and financial stability through digital entrepreneurship.

It isn't easy but it is fun. Take our example. A few years ago, both of us were traditionally well settled. I worked in a corporate job and Savi was completing her PhD. We had realized what we had set out to achieve, both in our educational journey and job-wise. We had well-paying jobs and a traditionally secure future ahead of us. But after exploring fifty-odd countries, we found ourselves falling more and more in love with the idea of travelling the world. Then, we quit our jobs to travel the world and pursue a career in digital media. After all, we get one life and the two of us wanted to enjoy every single sumptuous second of it.

This was not a whimsical decision. As you've read, it was part of a larger plan to hone our lives the way we wanted. That is why I always advise everyone, even friends and family, to conduct a little exercise. Every year, have an honest conversation with yourself about your goals and priorities. And when you do, do not let society's version of success cloud your vision. You might discover your definition of success is very different from society's mainstream version of success or even Bruised Passports' alternative version of success – you have your own unique definition, a composite of everything that makes you happy. This is why it is important to know your priorities clearly, without the fog of convention, and act on them.

Because the truth is, success is actually a heterogeneous concept, which means different things to different people. To some people it means being at the top rung of a corporate firm, to others it means being a millionaire. And there's nothing wrong with that at all! But success can also mean many other things – a peaceful life, a happy life and a content life. This happiness and, more importantly, contentment, is something that you consciously need to hone in your life. And that doesn't mean you're lazy! It just means you have different ambitions – the ambition for a slower life, a full life, a happy life spent appreciating the little things – home-cooked meals, stars in the sky, spending time with your loved ones!

That is the ambition that drives us. Losing Savi's dad, who was so dear to us, made us learn a crucial lesson – it is important to cherish the present because everything in life is fleeting. Once the shock of his passing had subsided, we decided to act on this lesson and make it an important part of our lives. Living in the 'now' can be all sorts of sensual and yet all of us spend all our time worrying about the future, which might not even happen. Cherishing the present, while working towards the future, has been the biggest game-changer on this journey of digital entrepreneurship for us. That is why advancing our careers while leading a joyous, fulfilling life each day is the goal we strive for.

Here's what we tell ourselves: let's say you have worked hard, you have prioritized a stable existence, you have even manifested abundance in every aspect of your life. What is the point if you do not enjoy every moment of it? For many, digital entrepreneurship is only about profits. But the true lure of location-independent entrepreneurship for us lies elsewhere – in the ability to programme our day according to ourselves and practise contentment in daily life. And by that, I don't mean slotting a meditation session into a busy day. I think our lives are much more fluid than that – we need to be conscious of what we put into our body and how we treat people around us. It is when we can eat the simplest of meals with delight and treat strangers with kindness, that's when we are truly successful! Our goal as content creators is to be able to balance a financially sustainable career with these things. Instead of always running after 'more'.

For me, it is this abandon; it is this luxury to go with the flow in a hyper-programmed world that is tantamount to success in the twenty-first century. As I voice this, I remember a stray evening on a little island in Fiji. The mere mention of Fiji invokes images of the bluest of beaches and vibrant marine life. But, for me, it is the traditional kava ceremony that cements the archetypal Fijian experience. Kava is a mild narcotic drink made from the crushed root of the *yaqona*. It is the national drink of Fiji and part of several ancestral and religious rituals in the country.

Our first communal kava ceremony was in the middle of the wilderness, in a small Fijian village. The drink is mixed in a large communal bowl, which is then passed around for everyone to sip from. We remember being sceptical when we took the first sip. We don't know whether it was the euphoric effects of the drink or the hypnotic strumming of guitars (Fijians love music!), but we found ourselves sucked into the communal ritual. We could feel our lips and tongues tingling and then going numb from the drink. Hours of singing and dancing later, many Fijians and visitors had left. But we were right there, yelling *Bula* (Fijian for 'hello') every time the bowl was passed on to us. Making friends with locals, partaking in ceremonies as old as time, being able to work from a remote island in Fiji – success!

10 . Savi and Vid: Dream a little, for good things are coming

Having established the importance of a stable model of income and hopefully given you some inspiration to achieve it in unconventional ways as well, let us come to the question we are most asked in real life, on social media and on our website. Why do we smile so much?

The truth is, it's neither a secret nor a magic pill. The reason is a conscious lifestyle choice that we've chosen to make over the past few years, and you can too. Some call it the Law of Attraction but it is simply the realization 'you become what you think'.

Let's start with the obvious. Despite what social media might portray, nobody's life is perfect and there are lots of niggles, ranging from mundane to severe, that everyone has to face. We have shared many of those during the course of this book. But you can choose to tackle them one way or the other. We live in an age where it is easy to be sucked into negativity. We have all had to face this at some point of our lives. But here's what we say: try ridding yourself of all negative thoughts for once. Jealousies, grudges, toxic people and negativity belong in the bin. This is not an overnight change but rather, a gradual process.

But you will be so much more creative if you have a happy mind full of positive thoughts. Instead of spewing venom, being envious, or thinking negatively about others, concentrate on working hard to be financially independent while realizing your dreams, however crazy those dreams might sound to other people.

This is not a cliché. It is something we have learnt from our journey – as we started to purge negativity from our lives, and got more and more passionate about creating high-quality content, things that used to bother us, didn't anymore. This nouveau entrepreneurship which focuses on generating an income and cultivating happiness comes with one condition – you need to stop judging others and encouraging negativity. This is your journey – prioritize happiness, contentment and those people in your life who love you as much as you love them.

Make a conscious decision to pursue this on getting up every single day. Once you have purged negativity from your life, it is time to start cultivating happiness and contentment. We do this in a variety of ways and so can you.

- Take joy in the small things – a home-cooked meal, a starry night, or the season's first snowfall.

- Work towards causes you are passionate about, for happiness is being able to channel your success to making others' lives better – for us, this is kids' education and women's empowerment

- Recognize the perfect in the imperfect. In life, as in travel, nothing is ever perfect. But looking at the glass half full, instead of half empty will change your life!

- Concentrate on having a wholesome soul and empowering the people around you, be it friends, family or co-workers, instead of bringing them down. And that is ALL you need for happiness and successes to come your way.

There is nothing we love more than helping you all who are reading this to reach out for your best life. We hope the little snippets we shared of the obstacles we've had to overcome in our lives will inspire you to carve a better future for yourself.

Whether you choose to be a digital entrepreneur or not, whether you choose to chase profit or happiness, whether you choose to travel or stay home, there are some things we would recommend to everyone. Live meaningfully, live consciously and stimulate your senses every chance you get – whether that is through reading, cinema or art! We will leave you with our favourite quote from Hemingway that will drive home the importance of truly relishing life: *Try to learn to breathe deeply, really to taste food when you eat, and when you sleep, really to sleep. Try as much as possible to be wholly alive with all your might, and when you laugh, laugh like hell. And when you get angry, get good and angry. Try to be alive. You will be dead soon enough.*

While the lake is the centre of Udaipur's attraction, make sure you see all the gorgeous historical monuments.

How can we n
include Paris in o
list of romantic citi

Christmas in Europe is so heart-warming, always.

If you want your fill of snow, and can't go to foreign lands, head to Gulmarg in Kashmir.

We loved our time hiking together on Meade Glacier in Alaska.

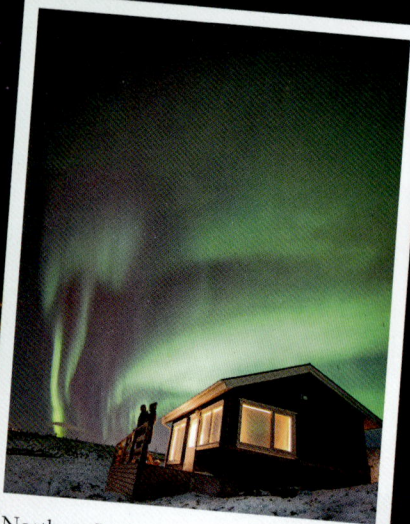

Northern Lights – the ultimate romantic experience to witness together.

The Ice Hotel in Lapland is a novelty experience you must not miss!

We loved being cosy in
an igloo in Finland.

Missing the vineyards of
France? Why not go to
Maharashtra instead?

South Korea is such an under-
appreciated destination, and we
loved every moment we spent there.

Dreamy Maldives –
should I say more?

Part 4

Romantic Trips

9

10 EPIC ROMANTIC GETAWAYS

Luxury traveller or backpacker, wine connoisseur or adventure enthusiast. I don't like typecasting travellers – every traveller is different.

Yet most people tend to envision a certain kind of holiday as soon as they hear the words 'honeymoon' or 'romantic getaway'. But not everyone wants to lay on a beach or sip a pina colada on their romantic getaway or honeymoon. The truth is, even the most romantic of getaways should be tailored according to the couple's personal tastes and preferences.

Keeping this in mind, here are ten incredible romantic getaways in India and abroad. There is something for you here, no matter what kind of traveller you are:

1. Luxurious privacy in the Maldives

If you want to spend your honeymoon marooned on a tiny island in the middle of the Indian Ocean, then there is truly no better place than the Maldives. The country offers some of the world's most luxurious getaways – you can spend all your time relaxing with your partner, indulging in watersports, getting massages under the Maldivian sun, trying out new wines, sampling eight-course meals, and relishing the privacy of its iconic overwater villas. This one is ideal for those of you who are looking for a truly relaxing getaway but do not have many days to spare.

2. Christmas markets in Europe

Nothing screams romantic like the cobbled streets of Europe, trees twinkling with fairy lights, and the spicy fragrance of mulled wine wafting through market squares. Christmas time is especially magical in Europe.

The weather can be a bit unpredictable but it is hard to argue with the prospect of quaint stalls lined with twinkling fairy lights, fairground rides, Christmas treats such as mince-pies, roast chestnuts and eggnog. Nearly all European cities have their own Christmas markets but we highly recommend Vienna's Christkindlmarkts, Prague's Wenceslas Square market and Nuremberg's Main Market Square.

3. *Old-school romance in Paris*

Paris is an elixir of sorts. It might be clichéd but this is a city where clichés converge to make magic happen. There is something so intensely magical about the city, even on the dreariest of days. Make sure you pepper your romantic getaway in Paris with uniquely Parisian experiences – go for a walk by the Seine. Have brunch somewhere on Rue de Montparnasse, an alleyway lined with crêperies by the dozen. Pick a selection of French pastries from a local patisserie such as Du Pain et des Ideés for an impromptu picnic after a morning of museum-hopping. Of course, no romantic getaway in Paris would be complete without a pit stop at the iconic macaron specialists – Ladurée.

Make sure you dine at as many cute French bistros as you can. If you enjoy French food, we highly recommend reserving a table at the much-acclaimed L'abeille.

If you have a few more days, you could also combine your Parisian rendezvous with a trip to the vineyards of Bordeaux and the coastal towns of the French Riviera.

4. Cultural gems and shopping in Seoul

Seoul might not be a destination that pops up on too many lists of romantic getaways, but if you ask us, it is ideal for a young couple that is curious about other cultures or heavily into Korean pop culture.

K-dramas and K-pop have taken the world by storm. Perhaps that is why one feels a strange sense of déjà vu upon entering a supermarket or exploring historical sites in Seoul. But fascination with Korean pop culture aside, Seoul is one of those cities that offers a mix of amazing food, fast public internet, friendly locals, lots of historical sites and a great vibe. Spend your days exploring historical palaces, trying Korean food, shopping your heart out and acquainting yourself with the hipster pockets of the city such as Ihwa Mural Village and Haneido. You might not know it, but Seoul is also a great place to see the iconic cherry blossoms bloom during spring months. This makes April an ideal month to visit. If you're after something different and thoroughly satisfying, this is it.

5. *Historical treasures in Udaipur*

India's hospitality is truly unparalleled. The country has some of the most beautiful hotels in the world, which are ideal for indulgent romantic getaways. Luxurious and scenic hotels combined with a history that dates back centuries makes Udaipur the ideal location for a truly romantic getaway.

Udaipur, fondly called the City of Lakes, is a stunning corner of Rajasthan that endears itself to most visitors. Make sure you enjoy your evening tea on a boat ride and linger over a lake-facing dinner. Spend your days walking through alleyways dripping with history, savouring delectable local delicacies, admiring colourful Rajasthan fabrics swaying in the wind and sharing tales with locals who greet visitors with huge smiles.

6. *An adventure of a lifetime in Alaska*

If you enjoy experiential getaways, then Alaska might be the one for you. It is not every day that you get to fly through fjords, spot humpback whales in the wild or canoe to ice walls and glaciers. But deep in the Alaskan wilderness, these are all things you will get to experience on a daily basis.

A romantic getaway in Alaska can be life-changing – looking at gargantuan glaciers and icebergs, it's easy to imagine the vast tundra that lies beyond the final frontier. Here, at the edge of the world, there is a surprise lurking around every corner. Entire valleys alive with bright pink flowers, mountains and landscapes draped with sapphire ice, whales and orcas playing and hunting in untouched wilderness, and glaciers by the dozen. There is something so incredibly seductive about nature this pristine, something that cannot be put into words.

7. Wine-tasting in Maharashtra

Undulating vineyards, memorable sunsets, nuanced wines, home-cooked Indian food and boutique accommodation – a vineyard stay in Maharashtra makes for a short and affordable weekend getaway.

Over the years, we've stayed in some great vineyard hotels in New Zealand, South Africa, Australia, the US and even Peru. But recently, we stayed at a vineyard in India for the first time and had a great weekend. We spent languid days biking around vineyards, making friends at the winery, observing the bottling process, driving around the Maharashtrian countryside and, most importantly, sampling an array of red wines, white wines and rosé blends. The months between August and March are ideal to visit these vineyards as they are lush green. You could also visit during harvest months – January to March – as the vineyards are laden with grapes and there are lots of events such as grape-stomping festivals and masterclasses scheduled for those months.

8. Something for all age groups in South Africa

This is the kind of romantic getaway that spurs couples to explore every nook and cranny of the world. It's tough to sum up a road trip through South Africa in a few words because it offers such a wide variety of experiences – safaris, vineyards, extreme adventure sports, turquoise beaches and much more.

We suggest spending a couple of days in Johannesburg before moving on to the iconic Garden Route. There is nothing it doesn't offer – great people, amazing panoramas, activities by the dozen, ambrosial wines and delectable seafood.

The Garden Route, traditionally, stretches between the Storms River and Mossel Bay. However, if you have a few extra days, we suggest an extended version of the traditional route starting from Addo Elephant National Park and ending at the wine routes around Cape Town. Along the way, you will get to visit colourful local markets, spot animals in the wild, have beach-facing breakfasts with penguins for company, indulge in adventure sports such as bungee jumping and sample a variety of South African wines. This is one romantic getaway we would recommend to anyone – young or old – in a heartbeat.

9. Relish the changing seasons in Kashmir

During the summer months, the orchards are in full bloom and hundreds of luscious red apples dangle precariously off trees. Juicy peaches being harvested; walnuts beginning to ripen in a nearby field. Hyacinths, irises and amaranth flowers lining roads that lead to snow-clad mountains. Come autumn, also known as *buen* in the area, Kashmir's iconic chinar trees change colour – expect a sea of ochres and yellows. And Kashmir's winter has an identity all its own – it enthrals and seduces in equal measure. Gulmarg is especially like a winter wonderland during the months of December and January.

Pick a season of your choice. But no matter what you pick, don't forget to take the time to talk to the people and listen to their stories. Kashmiris are warm and hospitable, and regale visitors with stories by the dozen. Of course, there is an unavoidable subtext of political conflict and violence that mars many a tale, but that is what makes interactions with locals in Kashmir so enlightening. In fact, these interactions will definitely be the highlight of your travels in the region.

In terms of sightseeing, you can choose from a variety of scenic and experiential excursions but we'd recommend sampling Wazwan cuisine in Srinagar, waking up early for the floating flower market, hopping on the Gulmarg Gondola, one of the highest operating cable cars in the world, hitting the ski slopes, or driving down to admire nature at Yousmarg.

10. Stare at the Northern Lights

Did we just save the most romantic experience of them all for the end? You bet! This is not a country-specific getaway, but an experiential one! The Northern Lights can be spotted between the months of October and February each year. Some of the best places to spot the Northern Lights are Scandinavia (especially Lapland, Norway and Sweden), Iceland, USA (Alaska) and Canada (Yukon, Yellowknife, Northern Labrador) and Russia (Murmansk and Arkhangelsk Oblast).

Watching the Northern Lights or the aurora borealis is definitely one of the most overwhelming travel experiences you will ever encounter. But since it is a natural phenomenon, it is hard to predict exactly when you will see the elusive green lights and how strong they will be. For this reason, we suggest not making this the sole aim of your holiday. Instead, plan a romantic winter holiday that also includes other novel experiences such as sleigh rides, visiting reindeer farms, snowmobiling on frozen rivers and staying in a heated glass igloo. This way you can enjoy your holiday while you consult the forecast and go hunting for aurora borealis. And chances are, you will spot them.

And when you do, expect to be stunned into silence. The Northern Lights can be overwhelming. The sky, dark one minute, is suddenly lit from within. They're on one horizon one minute and jump to another horizon the next. They're neon green, lime green, violet and pink all at once. We cried the first time we saw this show of nature and we're sure you will too.

EPILOGUE

They said love is fleeting, so we hung on to it through thick and thin.

They said marriage is about compromise, so we made it about equality.

They said jobs exist just to pay bills, so we made up one we enjoyed.

They said you need to settle for a mediocre life, so we made it about chasing the extraordinary.

xx
Savi and Vid

ABOUT THE AUTHORS

India's digital sweethearts and travel superheroes, **Savi Munjal** and **Vidit Taneja**, grew up in Delhi and, by now, have visited almost 100 countries together. Today, they are forerunners of the blogging and digital entrepreneurship sphere in India.

Over the past decade, they have mastered the art of content creation and storytelling on social media. As pioneers of professional travel blogging, they paved the way for location-independent entrepreneurship and encouraged many to make their passion their profession.

Bruised Passports (www.bruisedpassports.com, their official website), has won several awards from platforms such as *Outlook Traveller* and *Travel + Leisure* for their work. Their travel stories have also been featured on the Discovery Channel, National Geographic, CNN, *The Times of India*, *Hindustan Times* and the BBC, to name a few.